Text and images copyright © 2016
otherwise s

All rights re

Cover image designed by Graham Hodgson

Dedicated to Stan Coates, my fourth year junior school teacher who told me when I was eleven, "I shall expect to see your name in print one day, young lady".

Contents

Introduction 4

A brief history of travel. 8

Chapter 1   The South of France – Cap d'Agde and Canet Plage 15

Cap d'Agde – the return 28

Canet Plage 38

Chapter 2   Corfu: Kavos and Kanoni 42

Kanoni 50

Chapter 3   Mauritius 59

Chapter 4   Bali 78

Chapter 5   Gibraltar 104

Chapter 7   Amsterdam 118

Chapter 8   Fuerteventura 129

So where to next? 147

References and photo credits 148

Introduction

When I was growing up in the 60's, holidays were only for the rich. As a family we certainly weren't poor but we could never have afforded a holiday abroad.

Living at the seaside, we would spend time at the beach or playing tennis and having picnics with friends in one of our local parks. In those days we would see a lot of 'country folk' coming to spend a day or a week at the seaside, whilst those who lived at the seaside would go and spend time in the country.

As a family, we were very lucky; we had relatives who lived in the countryside. They were my paternal grandparents and early in the Second World War, they had been evacuated to a village called Dalston in Cumbria (or as it was known then, Cumberland), about 4 ½ miles from Carlisle. They decided to settle there and we used to spend between two and six weeks of the summer holidays with them.

At that time, Dalston was a very peaceful, pretty little village where everyone knew everyone else and they were all very friendly. If anyone felt homesick for the bright lights, noise and traffic there was a bus into Carlisle twice a week.

Dalston is still a very pretty village but it's much bigger and busier now.

The 50's and 60's were the heyday of the holiday camp and my Great Aunt once took me and my brother and sister to Butlin's at Filey for a week. There was certainly plenty to do but as I've never been much of a one for joining in, I probably didn't get the full benefit of it. I was happy just sitting reading.

'Auntie' also took the three of us to see the illuminations at Blackpool one weekend. We stayed at a small 'bed and breakfast' place and spent quite a lot of time wandering up and down the promenade and around the amusement arcades. As it was late October, it was too cold to be on the beach.

I remember that in the 1970's when I was at school, there were a couple of educational trips abroad and I have no doubt that had I wanted to go, the family would have found the money somehow but I didn't even consider it. I've always been a 'home bird' and never really wanted to be away from home for any length of time.

I have a vivid memory of being invited to a friend's house for a 'sleepover', long before they were called that. I think I was about eight. My friend's parents came to pick me up and drove me the three miles or so to their house. They were very nice to me and made me welcome but after about three hours, I decided I wanted to go home. I was happy to visit but I didn't want to sleep there, so eventually my friend's poor father had to get the car out and take me home.

My first holiday without the family came when I was about twenty and my husband and I went to Llandudno in North Wales for a week. We travelled there by coach.

We stayed in a small, seaside hotel only a few hundred yards from the beach and there was a cinema across the road. Of course, this was long before the days of the multiplex but the programme must have changed mid-week because I remember we went twice during our stay.

We had a few pleasant walks up a hill called the Great Orme and its little sister, the Little Orme. On the way back down on the far side of the hill, was a tiny church and a small graveyard. I wondered why they had been built in such an inhospitable place, halfway down a hill facing the sea.

In true holiday fashion, we went on a couple of day trips and visited places like Conwy Castle, the Snowdonia National Park and Portmerion, famous for its pottery and as the place where the 1960's cult television series 'The Prisoner' was filmed.

My favourite place was the beautiful Tudor mansion known as Gwydir Castle. The original house dates from 1500 and it had immaculately kept lawns and gardens where there were peacocks wandering around. Apparently, Gwydir was noted for its white peacocks, which I had never heard of up to that point. I suppose that goes to prove the old adage that travel broadens the mind.

I think it was this holiday that gave me my first sense of 'travel'. We stayed in a hotel, saw the local sights and explored the wider area and the local people even spoke a different language! I hadn't appreciated that people in North Wales speak Welsh but with a more English-sounding accent whereas people in South Wales speak English but with a Welsh accent.

I even came away with a couple of words of the local language, something that became a feature wherever I travelled after that. I learnt to say 'Bora da' (good morning) and 'Nos da' (good night) and most importantly, 'Cymru am byth', which means 'Wales Forever'. The language was way too complicated to learn much more than that!

Although I enjoyed my first visit to 'foreign parts', circumstances prevented me from making any further trips for a few years but then I met the man who became my second husband and constant travel companion. Thus began a series of holidays to various parts of the world and a lifelong love of travel.

As that great globe-trotter Michael Palin observed "Once the travel bug bites there is no known antidote and I know I shall be happily infected until the end of my life"

So fasten your seatbelt, make yourself comfortable and have a pleasant journey.

A brief history of travel.

It seems to me that since the birth of Thomas Cook in 1802, engineering, technology and fate conspired to ensure that only 150 years later, package holidays would begin to open up the world.

Although Thomas Cook can legitimately claim to be the father of the modern package holiday, other people and events played a significant role in making it possible to travel to almost anywhere in the world in less than a day and to spend time there.

Forms of transport have changed over the years and continue to get bigger, faster, more regular (unless you're trying to fly from Newcastle to Gatwick) and more luxurious. New countries have opened up to the traveller and as tourists, our tastes keep changing. We are more discerning; we want better food, more modern facilities, more comfortable accommodation and regular transport links to enable us to reach our destination more quickly.

It was all very different in the beginning.

In the 1800's, the only way of transporting people from one country to another was by sea and in 1819, the SS Savannah became the first dual steamer/sailing ship to cross the Atlantic carrying passengers. Due to the weather conditions, most of the journey was carried out under sail and the crossing took 27 ½ days.

This paved the way for larger and more regular Trans-Atlantic passenger-carrying services and gradually, ships became larger and more luxurious and included such famous liners as the Lusitania, the Mauritania and of course, the ill-fated Titanic which – for her very brief life – was the most luxurious ship afloat.

Once Trans-Atlantic flights became available, the popularity of the great ocean liners declined but in the 1970's there was a gradual resurgence of interest and the new cruise industry was born, allowing 'floating hotels' to carry passengers in comfort and luxury around the Caribbean, the Mediterranean the Baltic and elsewhere for periods of 7, 10, 14, 21 days or even longer.

The first iron steamship to go to sea was the 'Aaron Manby', which carried passengers and freight to France in June 1822 but the first cross-Channel passenger ferry was the English built paddle-steamer 'Rob Roy', which travelled to France on June 10th 1821.

Thus began a series of cross-Channel ferry links between such ports as Dover and Calais, Folkstone and Boulogne and Newhaven and Dieppe, managed by a small number of companies including P&O, Brittany Ferries and Townsend Thoresen, which owned the Herald of Free Enterprise. The 'Herald' capsized in 1987 with the loss of 193 passengers and crew. The company never recovered.

Thomas Cook organised his first excursion in 1841, when he took a group of fellow temperance league supporters from Leicester to Loughborough for a meeting. In 1845 he followed this with an organised excursion to Liverpool and Wales and in 1846 he began his regular and popular tours to Scotland.

This led the way for coach and rail companies to begin offering 'short breaks' to many parts of the UK and these are still popular today.

One of the most important requirements for the traveller is somewhere comfortable to stay and in the 1800's, two pioneers of luxury hotels were born. Cesar Ritz ('King of hoteliers and hotelier to Kings') was born in 1850 and Conrad Hilton was born in 1887. The first Hilton hotel was opened in Texas in 1925.

Across the world there are many hotels still bearing their names.

The majority of hotels are now owned by the large international chains but it is still possible to find some which are privately owned and managed. Many have been converted from castles, stately homes, hunting lodges, palaces and even monasteries and convents.

When international travel began to increase, there came the problem of currency. In the golden days before the Euro, all countries had their own currency but travellers crossing Europe often found themselves needing an extra holdall to carry the various notes they might need; Italy had the Lira, France had the Franc, Portugal had the Escudo, Greece had the Drachma and so on.

To combat this problem, in 1874 Thomas Cook introduced the 'circular note', the forerunner of the travellers' cheque. Travellers' cheques were a boon for tourists for many years as they meant it was no longer necessary to carry large quantities of cash when travelling abroad.

In the United States, dollar travellers' cheques could be spent just like currency without the need to cash them first.

In the 1990's with the increased use of credit cards, the advent of the Euro and the growth of the 'all inclusive' holiday, the use of travellers' cheques declined and it is now almost impossible to cash them, even at banks.

In the early 1900's, pioneers of a new and alternative form of transport appeared, with the first sustained aeroplane flight being completed by Orville Wright in 1903 and Charles Lindbergh's solo Trans-Atlantic flight from New York to Paris in 1927. Lindbergh's flight changed public opinion about air travel and this form of transport has become the mainstay of the modern package holiday.

I wonder if Lindbergh ever imagined that by the end of the century it would be possible to cross the Atlantic by plane in 3 hours! Did he ever think that it would be possible to access almost every country on the globe by aeroplane, albeit with the attendant frustrations of delays, cancellations and bureaucracy.

In the 1920's and 1930's it was only possible for the wealthy few to travel abroad. Most of the population still worked long hours and were poorly paid but in 1938 the 'Holiday With Pay' Act came into force, to the delight of the working classes and the disgust of many employers!

Even so, foreign travel was still out of the question for most people and even a holiday to another part of the UK remained a distant prospect. People used to have a day at the seaside or by the river and some went on 'working holidays' where they could go hop-picking in the countryside.

In the early 1900's, there was an organisation with the grand sounding name of 'Cunningham's Young Men's Holiday Camp', which was located at Douglas on the Isle of Man. Although accommodation was in tents, it could lay claim to being the first 'holiday camp'.

Cunningham's became an internment camp during the First World War.

In 1906, J Fletcher Dodd opened a holiday camp with hut-based accommodation and this led to the development of the company-owned holiday camps, which were popular in the 40's, 50's and 60's.

Harry Warner (founder of what is now the Warner Leisure Group), opened the first such holiday camp at Hayling Island in Hampshire in 1931. There is still a holiday camp at this site. Billy Butlin opened his first holiday camp at Skegness in 1936 and in 1946, the first Pontin's holiday camp opened at Bream in Somerset.

Such places were designed to appeal to all ages but especially to families and because food, accommodation and entertainment were all part of the package, they can be considered to be the forerunner of the modern 'all inclusive' holiday.

Nowadays, many people consider the holiday camps to have been rather regimented because activities and meals took place at specified times and as entertainment was available all day and into the evening, not a second was wasted but they were revolutionary in their day and brought family holidays into the reach of the masses for the first time.

These holidays also meant that families could spend a whole week together just having fun and enjoying themselves. Even today they remain a relatively inexpensive and popular option for a family holiday, although of course, there have been a number of concessions to modern tastes.

The advent of charter flights in the 1950's brought package holidays a step closer and the first charter flight from the UK took place in 1950 between Gatwick and Corsica, courtesy of a company called 'Horizon'. Horizon was to collapse spectacularly in 1974 – along with others in the Courtline group - leaving 40,000 UK holiday-makers temporarily stranded abroad.

The first modern package holiday took place in 1952 and the destination was Palma, Spain. Spain was the first mass package holiday destination and is still the most popular with British tourists.

The average cost of a two- week package holiday to Spain in the 1950's was £35 per person, which represented about 1/5 of the average annual salary but once there, food and drink were relatively cheap.

It was not until the 1970's that package holidays abroad started to become more affordable and popular with people in the UK. By the end of the 1970's, 2.5 million Brits had travelled abroad and by the end of the 1980's, this had risen to 10 million. The 80's also saw the start of the 'specialist' holiday, offering golf, ski-ing, long stay and of course, the infamous Club 18-30.

With larger aircraft and increased capacity – although not always greater comfort – long haul destinations such as the USA, Mexico, Canada and Australia became more popular and provided the intrepid traveller with seemingly endless possibilities.

By the mid-1990's the number of overseas holidays taken by UK residents had risen to 27 million.

Of course, with increased travel comes increased bureaucracy and in modern times, the ever-present threat of terrorist attack has led to a massive increase in security. This is a sad but seemingly inevitable consequence of modern life and most travellers accept it as such.

War, civil unrest and other factors mean that some areas of the world are no longer accessible – temporarily or otherwise – but the choice of destination has never been greater and the ease of travelling from A to B has improved considerably.

If space tourism becomes a reality for the earthbound traveller someday, it will be interesting to see what level of bureaucracy surrounds it and how this will be managed. After all, even the Apollo astronauts had to complete a US Customs Declaration when they returned from the Moon!

Chapter 1   The South of France – Cap d'Agde and Canet Plage

'Since life is short and the world is wide, the sooner you start exploring it, the better'   (Simon Raven)

It was August 1982 when I took my first holiday abroad. We went camping in the South of France. I must admit, it sounded very exotic. The rich and famous went there on holiday so I never thought it would be an option for the likes of me but the tickets confirmed it; I was going to the South of France. Monte Carlo, San Tropez, Monaco, Biarritz?

Our destination was Cap d'Agde and a private jet wasn't an option, we were going by coach. My travelling companions were my future husband Jimmy, my daughter Katherine – who was three years old – Jim's daughters Jane (14) and Victoria (12).

I hardly knew Jane and Victoria. They lived near Winchester and were at boarding school during term time so visits weren't that common. I wasn't sure how they'd feel about two interlopers encroaching on their 'Dad' time. Being close confined in a tent for two weeks was going to be a challenge for us all.

I have to admit, when the word 'tent' was first mentioned I had serious misgivings. Me? In a tent? Me??? I like my creature comforts, you see and I had visions of damp sleeping bags, uncomfortable ground sheets, buckets to bring water from the river and insects crawling all over.

Our journey from North East England was by coach, apart from the bit across the water which was by ferry and it took us 28 hours. The three girls slept most of the way. In those days, coaches didn't normally have videos to watch or toilets on board so there were frequent stops at various motorway service stations.

Again, motorway service stations weren't like they are now. These days they are like small shopping centres but back then, they were really just 'toilet stops', although if you were lucky, you could get a polystyrene cup of something that masqueraded as tea or coffee, or perhaps a bottle of Coca Cola and some sweets but that was about all.

Eventually, we arrived at the port of Dover, our gateway (or at least, waterway) to the continent and we sat and waited for the ferry to arrive. In the days before international terrorism and permanently heightened security, suitcases weren't taken off the coach and searched and neither was hand luggage and we just showed our passports to an official who came onto the coach for the purpose.

Passports in one form or another have been around since 450BC and in the UK, a passport in the form of a 'safe conduct' letter enabling an individual to travel across borders, dated from around 1414.

The forerunner of the modern passport dates back to 1914 and in the 1980's, it was still possible to travel abroad on what was called a 'Visitors Passport', which was basically a sheet of folded card containing a photo and the minimum amount of information. It was valid for a full year and I still have mine.

Meanwhile back at the port of Dover, the coach drove onto the cross-Channel ferry with all the passengers still on board and once we had reached our allocated place on the car deck, we were asked to leave the coach. I'm claustrophobic and I found it really unpleasant having to squeeze through rows of tightly packed cars and coaches so I was very relieved to find myself on deck.

Once in the open air, I got my first sight of the famous White Cliffs of Dover. I could almost hear Vera Lynn. It was one of those defining moments that I think every traveller has when they finally see something up close that prior to that time, they have only known through books, television and films. They're never how you imagined them to be; usually they're even better.

I was surprised how busy the Channel was; boats and ships of all sizes seemed to be dashing across the shipping lanes.

We disembarked at Calais which, in Tudor times, was a little piece of England on the continent but by the time I saw it, it was most decidedly French.

On our journey south there were a number of things to adjust to; not least of which was the traffic passing us on the 'wrong' side of the road. I was very impressed that our driver seemed equally at home driving on the left and the right. Roundabouts baffled me but fortunately, there weren't very many and I wasn't driving, so it didn't really matter.

I was also pleasantly surprised to discover that roads on the continent weren't covered in traffic cones all year round, unlike roads in Britain. The traffic must flow much more quickly!

The next adjustment was ordering coffee and doughnuts in French at one of the motorway service stations. Well, I managed to order coffee for us and orange juice for the girls but I wasn't sure my schoolgirl French was up to ordering much else. I was just relieved no-one wanted anything more complicated for breakfast!

I did a little better than the lady who was behind me in the queue. As we neared the counter I heard her ask her husband, "What's the French word for 'croissant'?"

The third aspect was the money. This didn't prove to be too difficult because in the days before the Euro, money was still worth something and every country had its own currency. In France, there were a hundred centimes to the Franc and ten Francs to the Pound Sterling, so even I could work out the price of everything.

It was a hot and sunny afternoon when we finally arrived at Les Sables D'Or (Golden Sands) campsite and I must confess, I was pleasantly surprised. There was a small shop, a play area for the children, a large wooden hut that turned out to be the multi-purpose clubhouse where the bar and evening entertainment were to be found and instead of the tiny, triangular tents I had expected, there were tidy rows of spacious ridge tents with separate sleeping spaces and a cooking/living area.

Now I should mention at this point that my husband can lay claim to inventing a very useful piece of equipment for campers and by the time our two- week holiday was over, nearly everyone on the campsite was using it.

There was a supply of candles in each tent because power cuts weren't unusual and after a day or two, nearly everyone had at least one empty wine bottle. The obvious thing was to jam the candle into the neck of the wine bottle so it could be used as a light on the outside table. Of course, the drawback was that the breeze would blow out the candle time and time again and people could use up an entire box of matches in one evening just trying to keep the thing alight.

The solution was simplicity itself, as most of the best ideas are. Take one plastic milk bottle, use the milk for its intended purpose then wash out the bottle. Turn it upside down and cut the bottom off then place the neck end of the bottle over the neck end of the wine bottle so that it surrounds the candle. Voila! A windproof, functional light which was diffused through the white plastic milk bottle and thus, gave a softer light.

I expect they're still in use today!

There was a generous amount of space between tents in order to provide at least some degree of privacy and outside of each tent was a table and several chairs. All meals were eaten at these tables and every night, campers would sit outside chatting, eating, drinking some of the local wine and perhaps playing cards……if they could still see them after a couple of glasses of wine!

The *'al fresco'* dining made it relatively easy for people to get to know at least some of their neighbours and of course, from day one all the children began to play together, not having the same inhibitions as their parents. By the second or third evening though, people began chatting and enjoying a glass of wine or two at each other's tables.

We got to know three families and we still have their photographs. There was a young-looking grandmother accompanied by her grandson and grand-daughter, a couple who had two young sons and another couple with two young daughters. I wonder what became of them all.

Some were there for two weeks, others only for a week. In the case of another family, one week was more than enough....at least for those of us who lived close by.

You might remember the Giles family, a cartoon series created by Ronald 'Carl' Giles for the Daily Express and which ran between 1945 and 1991 and which has continued in various annuals since then. If you don't know them, I'm sure Google can help.

Well, while we were staying at Les Sables D'Or, the Giles family also came to stay. They were in a tent diagonally opposite to us and about 20 yards away. There was Grandma, mother, father, 'teenage son' and 'teenage daughter'. It was obvious that they had arrived from the UK because their possessions were in supermarket carrier bags and 'father' was wearing a suit, shirt and tie. He wore them for the entire week, even on the beach!

Grandma had on a thick black coat and a black knitted beret (so clearly she knew she was in France) and she wore them every time she ventured outside the tent.

'Teenage daughter' soon discovered the delights of the disco in the clubhouse (yes, disco was really big in those far off days) and although it closed quite early because of the noise restrictions, she never arrived back less than an hour after closing time.

It was the same story every night. Around 11pm we would hear the zip around the tent flap open and then it would start; mother would shout, teenage daughter would shout then father would join in and within a couple of minutes there was a full scale screaming match. Why it never occurred to them to send one of their number to accompany her back from the disco each night, we couldn't fathom.

After about ten minutes, someone (we would take it in turns) would go across to their tent and politely ask them to keep the noise down because the children were asleep. The noise levels would then reduce to a low murmuring for a few minutes then gradually the volume would increase again.

One of the reps would appear and tell the family to stop disturbing everyone else. This normally produced results and everyone would settle down for the night.

After a couple of nights, people began to sit up late outside their tents and watch the drama unfold. Obviously there was no television so this became our nightly soap opera. Word spread and even people from other rows of tents would come and watch.

There was never any actual violence otherwise things would have been different and every morning they would all appear and carry on as though nothing had happened.

Our nightly entertainment came to a sudden and dramatic end on day six. It was early afternoon and most people were either making or eating lunch, when 'teenage boy' from the Giles family said something that sounded like "Ma; the tent's on fire". He said it in the same tone as he'd have asked someone to pass the salt and he didn't even look up from his comic.

Nothing happened so he decided to try the other parent. "Da; the tent's on fire".

By this time, several other campers had processed the information and while one man ran to notify the reps, the others grabbed the buckets of sand which were stationed outside of every tent for just such an emergency. They tried to extinguish the flames while Jimmy disconnected and moved the gas cylinder because if that had gone up, it would have levelled the campsite.

Mother and father didn't even get up from the table! Fortunately, Grandma was a bit quicker on the uptake and had brought their carrier bags out of the tent and placed them under the table. She then sat down next to the rest of the family and waited to see what would happen next.

Between them, three or four of the men and a couple of reps with fire extinguishers managed to put the fire out but by then, the tent had melted away and only the metal frame was left. The reps found another tent for the family to stay in for their last two nights and – having collected their plastic bags – they strolled off in single file to their new accommodation.

One thing that became clear to me very early on was that – spacious as the tents were – they did not have bathrooms *'en suite'* so ablutions had to take place in communal shower blocks with toilet facilities. The showers had separate cubicles thank goodness but frankly, showering anywhere amongst people of uncertain hygiene and in the company of several frogs (the amphibian kind; I'm not being disparaging about the French) is not my idea of the perfect holiday.

The first night I waited until I thought most people would have gone out for the evening or had at least, already showered, before I ventured in. I didn't hang about though;

as well as the frogs, there were way too many moths for my liking.

Wending my way back to the tent in the dark – especially after the blinding lights in the shower block – was a bit of an ordeal but eventually I made it. No-one was more surprised than me to discover that I had arrived back at the right tent!

I was greeted by Jimmy, who was having a laugh at my expense. He said "You must have tripped over every guide rope on the way back. It sounded like someone playing the harp!" After two or three nights I became quite proficient at it!

Only a couple of hundred yards away from the campsite and accessible by a narrow dirt track with small vineyards on either side, was the large, sandy beach. Jimmy took the girls down one morning. It was a warm day; sunny but very windy.

As they walked along the water's edge, they saw several people aboard a beautiful cabin cruiser, some distance from shore. They were waving and shouting " 'Allo, 'allo" so the girls waved back and shouted "Hello". (You see the subtle difference in the language there?).

After a minute or two, Jimmy noticed that the prow of the boat appeared to have taken on a life of its own whilst the stern remained stationary and he suddenly realised that it had run aground on the rocks. The people on board were waving and shouting for help!

He ran across to the lifeguard station and tried to tell them what was happening but he doesn't speak French. Being a real Geordie he still struggles with English, so he had to point outside and eventually, one of the lifeguards followed him to the door. Jimmy pointed to the stricken boat. The lifeguards hadn't seen it because it was around the outcrop of rocks that jutted from the beach into the sea.

The lifeguards brought out their inflatable boat and set off to rescue the stranded sailors. They survived their ordeal but I can't say the same for their boat.

One evening there was a children's fancy dress competition at the clubhouse and we struggled to think of a suitable costume for Katherine. We hadn't brought anything with us so we had to improvise. Eventually we found a clean, black plastic refuse sack and the two older girls were set to work to find 'clean' rubbish, such as washed out milk cartons, sweet wrappers, labels from tins.

I spent the afternoon sticking, pinning and sewing the rubbish onto the refuse sack then Jimmy cut holes in it for Katherine's head and arms to go through and she went dressed as a litter bug. She wasn't exactly thrilled about it.

On the way to the clubhouse, we came across several young people throwing buckets of water over each other. Thinking it was just youthful high spirits and secure in the knowledge that they wouldn't throw water at tourists who had got dressed to go out for the evening, we continued walking.

Seconds later, the contents of half a barrel of water were heading in our direction. I dodged most of it and just got splashed as the water hit the ground but Jimmy caught most of it head on. He was not amused and had to go back to the tent to change.

On the plus side, Katherine won first prize in the fancy dress competition. Her prize was a giant bar of chocolate, so that soon cheered her up.

Later as we were talking about the water incident, Jimmy told me that he had asked one of the reps what it was all about and the rep said that it was to do with the burning of Joan of Arc. Apparently, the water represented the symbolic dousing of the flames, as the peasants had tried to do at the time.

On our 'second from last' night when we were sitting around the table with some of our neighbours, the conversation once again turned to the 'water' incident and someone asked why people did that. I confidently explained the symbolic dousing of the flames which had consumed Joan of Arc and it seemed to make perfect sense to them, as indeed it had to me.

Jimmy started to laugh. He said he didn't know what it meant either but that he'd made up the Joan of Arc story. It was my turn not to be amused. To this day we don't know whether there was any real reason for the ritual soaking of groups of unsuspecting tourists.

On our last night in Cap d'Agde, about ten of us gathered around a couple of tables after the children had gone to bed and we chatted whilst finishing off the last of the wine we'd all bought during our stay.

Several local winegrowers had formed themselves into a co-operative and combined the grapes they grew to produce their own 'brew' and it was possible to purchase copious amounts for very little money. The most common container was a plastic half gallon or one gallon one and we purchased a half gallon of a rather palatable, light red for ten Francs.

Now I've always been a bit of a lightweight when it comes to alcohol consumption and in those days, I hardly ever had a drink so even the four pints in our plastic container was a lot for me to shift in a fortnight. I still had about half of it left that evening. Most of us had some red or white wine left and a few of the men had some beer so after a couple of hours in convivial company, we had managed to make most of it disappear.

It was at that point that someone produced the remains of a bottle of Duty Free gin. Oh dear. I didn't know about mixing drinks in those days and I certainly wasn't a gin drinker so I only had one glass. Big mistake.

The evening wound up at about 10.30 and we all dispersed to our own tents. I felt fine….until I lay down. I was suddenly aware of a very strange and rather unpleasant sensation; the tent appeared to be spinning!

Not knowing what it meant, I turned over onto my left side and it happened again. I lay on my back and tried to focus on a fixed point in the tent but none of the points seemed to be fixed any more.

I sat up and the spinning stopped. With a sigh of relief, I lay back down only for the spinning to start again. I decided that what I needed was some fresh air so I got up and went outside to sit at the table for a while. I sat resting my head on my arms and that seemed to help a little.

Eventually, Jimmy came out to see where I was. He took one look at me and said – not without some sympathy – "Look at the state of you. We've got a thirty-hour journey tomorrow and you're going to be ill."

After a few hours the feeling subsided sufficiently for me to go back to bed and I managed to have a few hours of sleep. I emerged around ten o'clock the next morning feeling as fresh as a daisy!

It was just as well really because apart from the journey, I had all the packing to do.

Our thirty- hour journey was completed without incident and more importantly, without any ill effects.

Cap d'Agde – the return

We returned to Cap d'Agde a couple of years after our first visit but this time we went a little 'up-market' and stayed in a large, static caravan; what's referred to today as a mobile home, although it wasn't mobile. It was comfortable and had almost every amenity we could want.

One thing we discovered it didn't have was an ice cube tray so we tried to improvise, without much success. It was Katherine who came up with the solution.

She took the tray of eggs that had been in our 'welcome pack' and put the eggs in a bowl. She asked "Will this do? You can put water in it where the eggs were." The tray was plastic so Jimmy cut off the lid and filled one half of the container with water then put it in the ice box.

A few hours later, there they were; six unusually shaped but perfectly useable ice cubes!

Jimmy and Katherine used to go and buy the fresh bread every morning and evening. The three of us used to go for the other shopping, as I could remember a little of my 'schoolgirl' French; although we did live on ham, cheese, bread, tomatoes and chips for a few days until I gained some confidence.

Jimmy did all the cooking and we ate very well, enjoying meals of steak or chicken most nights. Occasionally, the steak or chicken would be further enhanced by the addition of copious amounts of red wine, generously supplied on a regular basis by one of our neighbours.

His name was Jean-Marc and Jimmy and his daughters had met him on a previous visit when Jean-Marc was there with his daughters. Jean-Marc had invited them to his caravan for dinner one night and he noticed that Jimmy wasn't drinking much wine. When asked why, Jimmy made the sacrilegious remark that he didn't really like wine, so Jean-Marc brought out another bottle for him to try.

It was then that Jimmy discovered his love of Pernod.

The year that Katherine and I went back, Jean-Marc and his girls were there too. They came to see us one day and between his broken English and my fractured French, we just about managed to communicate.

Our friend presented us with several bottles of red wine, which I must say, were delicious. There were no labels on the bottles so we assumed that like most of us, he had the bottles 'topped up' with the locally produced wine at the co-operative van. I drank some of the wine but quite a bit was added to whatever we were having for dinner each evening.

On the last day of his holiday, Jean-Marc and the girls came to say their goodbyes and he gave us another three bottles of wine because he didn't want to take them back home again. I commented that the wine was very good and he said (in French, of course) that it was Beaujolais. I responded that yes, it was very much like Beaujolais (not that I would have known the difference between one red wine and another).

He said "Oui, c'est Beaujolais" and he produced his business card. As I read it I realised what he was saying. He and his family owned vineyards near Lyon where the grapes were grown to make Beaujolais and what we had been drinking and pouring onto our dinner every night, was wine from his own vineyards. Obviously they hadn't put labels on the bottles that were for their own consumption.

Needless to say, the remainder of the wine was sipped and savoured rather than forming a sauce for our food.

One day, Jimmy took the girls down to the beach while I wrote post cards and when they returned a couple of hours later, he asked if we had a large pan to cook the mussels he'd caught. I found the biggest pan we had and he produced a bucketful of mussels.

Apparently, it had been pretty tiring work because he had to snorkel down to where the mussels were several times and it had taken him most of the morning.

Katherine and I don't eat seafood or shellfish but Jimmy and the girls like it so he set about cooking the mussels for their lunch whilst regaling us with tales of fighting off giant squid and the ever present danger of shark attack. Well, maybe that was a slight exaggeration.

It turned out that he had bought the mussels from a fisherman on the beach and he was the one who had actually done all the hard work of catching them.

One evening while we were preparing dinner, Victoria was complaining of earache so I thought that some warm oil might help. I knew we had some olive oil and suggested that warming a spoon and putting a few drops of oil on would probably be the easiest way to do it.

I brought out the oil and began heating some water in a pan to warm the spoon. I went to the cupboard to find some cotton wool. In the meantime, Victoria brought the spoon over to me. It had some oil on so I said I'd test it to make sure it wasn't too hot. I put the pad of my little finger in the oil and screamed in agony. It was boiling!

Apparently she had put the oil on the spoon and heated it in the gas flame. If she had poured it in her ear it would have killed her.

I escaped with a huge white blister on my finger and I had to sit with it in a glass of iced water for the rest of the evening. Every time I took my finger out of the ice, the pain was excruciating.

A few days later, we had a walk to the marina at Cap d'Agde and spent a couple of hours looking at the beautiful yachts and boats and visiting several rather smart shops.

Cap d'Agde became a tourist resort in the 1970's and grew rapidly. Although it now has a lot more shops and even a golf course, the marina was the main attraction in the 1980's. It soon became known as a nudist and naturist resort, too. Just as well the weather is usually hot and sunny!

One day as we headed back to the campsite, we noticed the sky beginning to darken quite considerably and soon it was obvious it was going to rain very hard, very soon. We began to hurry but it was clear we weren't going to be able to outrun it. We were going to get a soaking!

The sky began to turn dark green and then the storm began. We heard the rumble of thunder coming ever closer and then the lightening started. The thunder turned from rumbles to loud cracks overhead and the rain became so heavy that it couldn't drain from the road fast enough and soon became a stream. Before long we were ankle deep in rainwater.

The sudden change in the weather had caught a lot of people unawares; there were maybe fifty or sixty people hurrying ahead of us, trying to reach their campsites and almost as many behind us trying to do the same.

Suddenly, I saw the lightening up ahead. It hit the road twenty or thirty feet in front of us – a bright green spark – then 'bounced' along the road three or four times, each bounce bringing it nearer and nearer. It was heading straight for us and I just stood there, paralysed with fear. The girls were screaming and I really thought we'd had it.

The last spark hit the ground about ten feet in front of us and then it stopped. I'm convinced that I've never been closer to death than I was that day.

As the storm continued, local people and those from nearby campsites who had cars (mostly French people), would stop and pick up storm-drenched campers and drop them off at their respective campsites.

One very nice French lady in a beautiful white Mercedes, stopped next to us and told us to get in the car. We were worried about ruining the upholstery because the rain was running off us in torrents but she was insistent. About ten minutes later, we were dropped off at Les Sables D'Or.

What we saw made us very glad we were staying in a caravan.

All the tents had been flooded out and men were frantically digging trenches around the tents to catch the rainwater but they weren't having much success. The power was off and remained so for several hours.

Most of the caravan-dwellers tried to help by inviting the tent-dwellers in out of the rain, providing them with towels to dry off and making them cups of tea or coffee. The clubhouse opened its doors early so people could shelter there, store their belongings and wait for the power to come back on. Fortunately, the clubhouse had its own generator.

The storm raged on for another hour but the next day, it was bright, sunny and warm, as though the storm had never happened. There was a huge clean- up operation but everyone 'pitched in' and helped where they could and by that evening, everything was pretty much back to normal.

Two or three times during the holiday we walked into the walled town of Agde. Agde is 466 miles from Paris and is one of the oldest towns in France. Originally a Greek city, the site has been occupied since 526 AD. Although it looks quite small, there is a population of around 23,000.

It's a very picturesque place with lots of narrow, cobbled streets and lots of lovely old buildings, many of which were constructed from the distinctive black basalt from the nearby Mont Saint-Loup volcano.

There was – and I believe, still is – a market twice a week, selling a range of goods from flowers and locally grown produce to tourist souvenirs and traditional crafts. We would visit Agde in the morning because later in the day, the temperature became very hot and it was quite a long walk from the campsite.

In the early evening, we would sometimes have a much shorter walk to the local fishing village of Grau d'Agde. Although the village has accepted tourism, it has not allowed tourists to ruin the traditions and personality of the village;

as a result, it has not suffered the fate of many former fishing villages elsewhere in the world (Kavos on Corfu, for example).

Whilst there are a number of restaurants along the shore and they provide fresh and delicious food to tourists and locals alike, Grau d'Agde remains at heart, a traditional fishing village with well-maintained old buildings and its old traditions.

Whilst staying at Cap d'Agde, we took the opportunity to see a bit more of the countryside and opted for a day trip to visit the caves at Clamouse. The caves form part of the Gorges de l'Herault in the Languedoc region and were discovered in 1945. They are located almost two miles from the beautiful medieval village of Saint Guilhem le Desert, which we also visited.

The guided tour of the caves – which stretch for just over half a mile – took about an hour to an hour and a quarter and the stalactites and stalagmites are spectacular. Often nature's creations are at least as magnificent as anything created by the hand of man.

As with most holidays, they come to an end much too soon and after two weeks, we clambered aboard our coach once more for the homeward journey.

As we travelled north, the coach driver advised us that because of traffic delays *en route*, we would miss the ferry we were booked on so rather than having us sit and wait at the ferry terminal, he would detour and take us into Paris where we could have some time to wander around.

It was late at night and Paris was lit up like a Christmas tree. It was beautiful. Somehow the driver managed to park in the city centre for an hour and everyone got off the coach to have a walk around and enjoy – albeit briefly – Paris by night.

Jimmy's reason for leaving the coach was rather more prosaic but necessary. His elder daughter Jane had lots of insect bites on her legs and she was in some discomfort so he, Jane and Victoria went off in search of a pharmacy.

Katherine was fast asleep on my knee and totally oblivious to the fact we were in Paris. I wouldn't have left her alone on the coach, even sleeping, so my first – and so far, only – sight of the Champs Elysses, the Arc de Triomphe, the Eiffel Tower and the lights of Paris were through the windows of our coach.

It was still beautiful and the perfect end to our holiday in the South of France. Who knows, maybe someday I'll have the opportunity to experience Paris again but next time, up close.

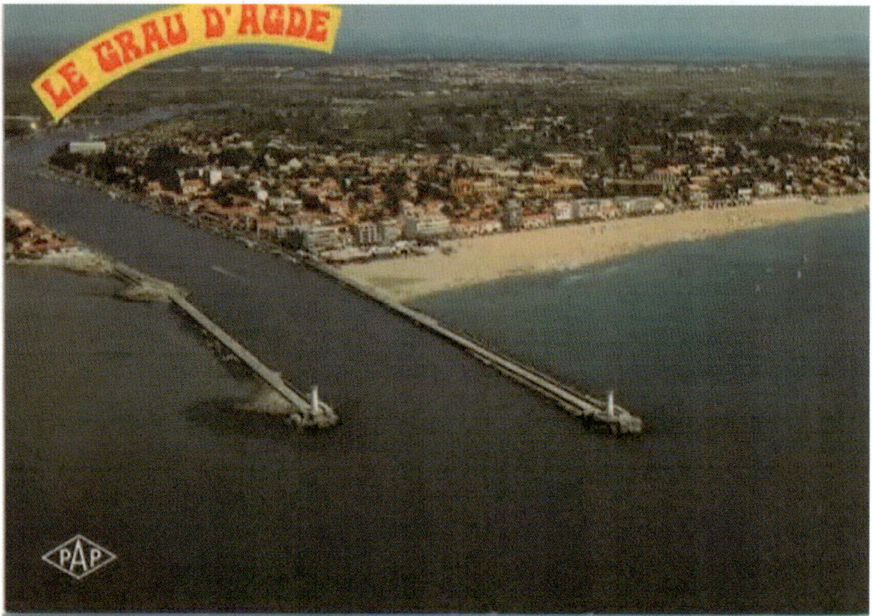
LE GRAU D'AGDE
PAP

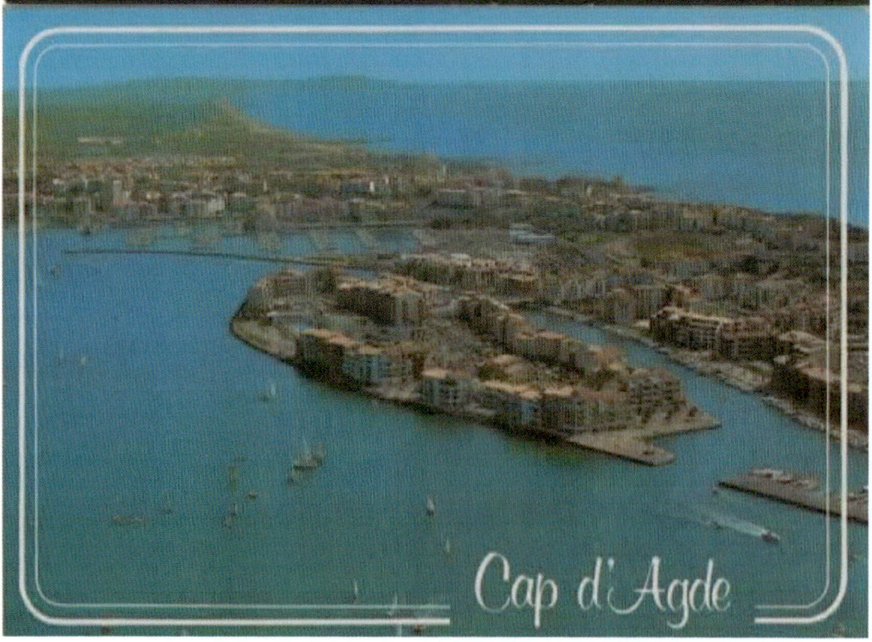
Cap d'Agde

Agde

Canet Plage

A couple of years after our last visit to Cap 'Agde, we returned to the South of France, this time without Jane and Victoria but with my mother. She had been unwell for a while and Dad thought it would do her good to have a holiday in the sun. It was her first trip abroad and we were to be away for three weeks.

We stayed in a caravan at a campsite called Mar Estang in the resort of Canet Plage. The resort is located near Perpignan and is close to the Spanish border. The area is well-known for the Canet Saint-Nazaire nature reserve, with its pink flamingos.

The campsite backs onto the lake where the flamingos would gather just before sunset. There was a wooden viewing platform from which to get a better view but it had a hole in the corner that hadn't been roped off or repaired and Katherine managed to fall through it.

Her legs were grazed and bruised – as they usually were – but otherwise she wasn't badly hurt. Katherine has always been a bit of a klutz; she still is. She has the ability to trip over a shadow and furniture regularly jumps into the middle of the floor just so she can trip over it.

One of the bedrooms in the caravan had bunk beds. Mam slept in the bottom one and Katherine slept in the top. In the early hours one morning, there was a tremendous thud and we rushed in to find that Katherine had fallen out of bed. Again, she wasn't hurt, probably because she was sound asleep when she hit the floor.

To this day, Jimmy refers to it as "Katherine's early morning fall".

At that time the campsite (like many others) had little in the way of facilities but the caravans were clean and comfortable. There were shops close by and it was only a few minutes' walk to the beach, which was accessed through a tunnel that ran under the main road.

There was an enormous stretch of beach and Mam – who had only recently learned to swim – would spend a lot of time in the sea. There was a long, modern promenade and most evenings we would have a walk along it after dinner.

The campsite at Mar Estang now has a five-star rating and contains many more facilities including swimming pools, restaurants, a fitness room, disco, hairdresser and tennis courts.

We decided that we would go on at least one trip while we were there, so we chose Andorra. Andorra is most famous as a winter ski resort but in the summer, it is possible to walk the slopes and take the ski lifts to the peaks.

Our journey took us through some beautiful towns and villages and lovely countryside and we made a couple of stops to have a look around. The journey takes between two and three hours, depending on traffic.

There was often a queue at the border because in those days, there was only one official on duty. If he happened to be on his lunch break it was necessary to go and find him in order that passports could be checked and stamped.

The day we were there, the queue was quite lengthy so the passports were just glanced at and not stamped, which we were very disappointed about.

The principality of Andorra was founded in 1278 and covers an area of about 180 square miles between France and Spain. The official language is Catalan but because of its location, French and Spanish are widely spoken. Surprisingly, Portugese is spoken there, too.

Although Andorra is not part of the European Union, the currency is the Euro and there are many designer and tax free shops in which to spend your Euros. Around ten million visitors travel to the principality every year, mostly in the winter.

The capital – Andorra la Vella – is the highest capital city in Europe at 3356 feet above sea level and this is clearly beneficial to the local residents, who enjoy one of the highest life expectancies in Europe at 81 years.

After three weeks of relaxation, we had to say goodbye (or perhaps, 'au revoir') to Canet Plage and begin the long journey home. The cross-Channel part of the journey was pretty hair-raising because we caught the tail end of Hurricane Katrina and the Channel was churning.

Our ferry took a real pounding and in spite of the stabilisers, the ship rolled and pitched throughout the entire journey. No-one was allowed on deck and people sat where they could, mostly on the floor or the stairs because standing was quite hazardous. People standing or walking were being thrown around and several lost their balance entirely. A couple of passengers fell down a small flight of stairs but fortunately, they weren't badly hurt.

The sight of the English coast was quite a relief but it also heralded the end of another holiday.

By then though, I had been bitten by the travel bug. Having had my first taste of foreign travel in various parts of the South of France, I couldn't wait to see what else the world had to offer.

The promenade at Canet Plage

Chapter 2   Corfu: Kavos and Kanoni

'The world is a book amd those who do not travel read only one page'   (St Agustine)

Kavos

Ever since I read Gerald Durrell's book 'My Family and Other Animals' I had wanted to visit Corfu.

It was the first time I had read such a book because it seemed to be three stories in one; the hilarious adventures of the family and the people they met, the detailed description of the local fauna and flora by the budding naturalist and the vivid descriptions of the beauty of the island, with its bright colours and quaint locations.

Of course, Gerald Durrell and his family lived on Corfu in the 1930's; a lot of things had changed by the time I arrived 50 years later, though fortunately, not everything.

Corfu (in Greek, 'Kerkyra') is located off the north west coast of Greece in the Ionian Sea. It was first settled in the 8th century and has at various times been ruled by Italy, France and Britain but on the 21st May 1853, the British handed Corfu back to Greece to be ruled by the new monarch, King George 1st of Greece.

Corfu was one of the first of the Greek Islands to embrace tourism (often to its own detriment) and it remains a popular destination for British holidaymakers. Amongst the party towns, it is possible to find plenty of quiet, peaceful, unspoilt places to enjoy.

Corfu's first real 'party town' was Benitses, which we passed through in the coach on the way from the airport. It was almost deserted and very quiet but of course, it was lunch time so more than likely, everyone was still sleeping off the previous night's excesses.

My first ever flight on an aircraft was to Corfu. It was one of the relatively few places that could be reached from our local airport (Newcastle) at that time.

I remember being very impressed that shortly after we had taken off, we were served with breakfast and actually, it was very nice. We had a roll and butter with marmalade, orange juice, coffee and a little tin tray containing scrambled egg, sausage, tomato and beans. I enjoyed it, which is more than I can say for most of the in-flight catering I've experienced since then!

The view from the aircraft window was amazing; flying over France, over the snow-capped Alps and seeing the tiny villages below us, Italy and the beautiful blue Mediterranean......it was spectacular!

Having negotiated Greek passport control without any difficulty, we stepped into the heat of an August day and were pointed in the direction of our coach. I took in as much as I could of the views of the countryside and tried to see it as Gerald Durrell might have seen it. There was still enough of 'old Corfu' left for me to do that and I could see at least some of what he saw.

The coach dropped us off on the side of the narrow road, seemingly in the middle of nowhere. We followed a dirt track until we arrived at a large, two-storey building with magnolia coloured walls and green shutters. It was – I discovered – a fairly common design for houses and there were lots of them dotted all over the island.

The building had been turned into three self-catering apartments; one upstairs, one downstairs and a third smaller one at the side. We had the downstairs one. The rooms were large and sparsely furnished but comfortable. Unfortunately, there was no air conditioning but there was a veranda front and back which looked onto the olive groves and the small field full of fruit trees. There was also a large kitchen and two bedrooms. It was the first time Katherine had had a bedroom of her own on holiday so she was quite excited about that.

Although we had booked our holiday through a travel agent (no internet back then!), the villa itself was privately owned by a very nice man called Spiros. Most men on Corfu are called Spiros after their patron saint, Saint Spiridion.

Spiros lived nearby with his beautiful wife Maria and their daughter, Anna. Anna was ten years old, only two years older than Katherine and the girls used to play together almost every day.

Maria came every morning to clean the three apartments. She spoke no English and my knowledge of Greek was limited to the ancient Greek alphabet which I had been taught at Grammar School, so that wasn't much help. Fortunately, Anna spoke a little English and would translate. I managed to pick up a couple of words of Greek during our stay; just enough to say 'good morning', 'how are you', 'please', 'thank you' and 'hello' but that was enough to get by, especially when we went shopping.

Shopping was a problem for the first couple of days because although we had a 'welcome pack' of essentials sufficient for the first day and we had brought a coolbag of things from home (you could do that in those days), we needed to stock up on other consumables and the nearest shops were in Kavos itself.

According to the brochure, it was only a 'ten to fifteen-minute walk' into Kavos so early the next morning, Jimmy and Katherine set off for the shops. I expected them back within the hour so when two hours had passed, I was beginning to grow concerned. About half an hour later, they returned.

The 'ten to fifteen -minute walk' that the brochure promised turned out to be a forty minute walk each way. Well, it was one thing to walk into town but it was quite another having to walk back with heavy bags full of shopping, so we decided to call into the portacabin which was occupied by a variety of reps and ask them to explain.

Apparently we weren't the only ones to have something to say about this so after a couple of days, head office approved an amount of money so that people could get taxis to bring back their shopping. We didn't abuse it; we used to walk into town and just get the taxi back when we had heavy shopping to carry.

We had a nice young couple living next door and they had hired a moped. Every day – until the taxi service had been approved – they would ask us if there was anything we needed from the shops and if we needed anything heavy – such as bottles of lemonade – they would bring it back for us. It was very kind of them.

Back then, Kavos was quite a pretty, very quiet fishing village with some nice little shops and a lovely stretch of beach. We would sometimes walk in in the early evening, have a look around and walk back. We always took a torch with us to light our way along the road because it got dark very quickly and there were no street lights. The evenings were warm so it was quite a pleasant walk.

One aspect of Corfu that I quickly came to detest was the nightly arrival of the mosquitoes.

As soon as I got into bed and lay down, a mosquito would appear. That horrible, high pitched 'hum' would wizz past my ear time and time again until it nearly drove me mad! Of course, as soon as one of us put on the light, the evil little thing would disappear but I knew that it was hiding behind the headboard laughing because as soon as the light went off again, it would reappear.

If we managed to see one of these horrible creatures on the wall, Jimmy would kill it and with a sigh of relief, I would lie back down and try to go back to sleep, only to have another mosquito appear! I swear they used to take it in turns to annoy us.

When we returned the following year we were armed with several plug-in mosquito repellents. They seemed to do the trick.

One night after we had done battle with a couple of these tormentors, I was about to turn out the light when I noticed something on the floor that hadn't been there before. I picked up my glasses to take a better look and to my horror, I recognised it as a scorpion! I'd never actually seen a scorpion up close before, so part of me was curious and I sat looking at it for a few minutes.

It sat looking at me too, so we had a bit of a stand-off for a while but eventually, I decided that – interesting though it was – I really wasn't prepared to share a room with it so of course, Jimmy had to get up and deal with it.

He doesn't normally like to kill creatures (apart from mosquitoes) so he found a cloth and persuaded the scorpion to scuttle onto it, then he went to the veranda and shook the cloth and its contents into the field.

In spite of our battles with the local wildlife, we had a lovely, peaceful and relaxing holiday in Kavos. In fact, we liked it so much we decided to go back the following year. That was a huge mistake and it left us dealing with wildlife of an entirely different sort.

In the space of a year, Kavos had turned from 'peaceful fishing village' to 'party city' and to this day, it has a reputation (entirely justified) for attracting those of the 'lager lout' mentality. These are people who believe that you have to spend money to go on holiday in order to stay so drunk for two weeks that you can't remember having been away at all.

Recently the local residents have begun to complain about the drunkenness and bad behaviour, which I find very ironic. They've put up with it for 30 years and have taken all the money it brought in without complaining, so what right have they to complain now? They actively encouraged it and failed to set boundaries or take action.

We were fairly lucky in that we were staying in the same apartment as the previous year, about forty minutes from the madness of Kavos itself. Early in the holiday, we walked into town to find that nearly all the shops had closed and most had been turned into bars or discos. Nearly every bar and disco had enormous speakers outside and the noise was deafening! After that we only ventured in during the day while the drunks were sleeping off their hangovers and only then, when it was necessary to get some shopping.

Going into town in the evening had become perilous for another reason, too. There were no street lights, road markings or pavements but even if there had been, most of the young people on scooters and mopeds were so drunk they probably couldn't have seen them anyway!

Even our lovely, quiet apartment nestled between the olive groves and fruit trees, had gone. The olive groves and fruit trees had been replaced by other two storey apartments and a swimming pool. There was music playing by the pool all day and into the evening, even during the Greek 'siesta time'.

Late at night, a dozen or so alcohol-fuelled young people would arrive from Kavos on their mopeds and spend a noisy hour or two jumping in our pool and screaming and yelling.

Spiros had his hands full trying to manage the holiday complex and Maria and her daughter were both on cleaning duty so we hardly saw them. We were shocked when we saw Maria because in the space of a year, she had turned from a very attractive young woman into what can only be described as a drudge. She had aged about twenty years and looked exhausted, pretty much as I did by the end of that holiday!

For the only time in my years of travelling (at least, so far) I couldn't wait for the holiday to be over and to get home. Gerald Durrell would have been spinning in his grave, except that he wasn't dead at that point.

Would we ever return to Kavos? Never!........unless it goes back to being a small, quiet fishing village with a 4 or 5 star hotel!

Typical house design on Corfu.

Kanoni

Our last visit to Corfu – at least to date – took place in 1993 and came about by accident.

We had planned to go to Florida with Katherine and my parents but for several months, there had been disturbing reports in the media of tourists in Florida being targeted and shot. It had reached such proportions that many people – including ourselves – decided they weren't prepared to take the risk and cancelled their holidays.

We decided that instead of cancelling altogether and losing our money, we would choose another destination. Our options in terms of flying from Newcastle Airport were limited but eventually we chose Corfu.

Of course, we had to get ourselves into the mindset of having a holiday on Corfu so that we wouldn't spend the entire fortnight thinking "We should be in Florida". We were staying at the Hilton, so we assumed that the food and accommodation would be good.

Our flight was on Ambassador Airlines, which unfortunately ceased operations the following year but I'm sure that had nothing to do with us. It was a night flight so unfortunately we couldn't see the beautiful scenery on the way to Corfu.

We arrived at the airport at around 10.30pm and Dad had his suitcase within ten minutes but in the way that these things normally work, we had to wait another half an hour for the other three.

The hotel was right next to the airport; in fact, the runway cuts across the end of the beach and we often used to watch the planes landing and taking off. My mother loves planes so she was quite happy to sit and watch them, day or night and she never seemed to mind the noise.

Kanoni was once the capital of Corfu and the name itself means 'cannons', a reference to the cannons which were positioned in the area to guard the main port.

After breakfast on our first morning, we decided to go for a stroll and see a little bit of the local area. After about an hour we arrived at a picturesque marina, where we sat and had a cold drink. During this brief interlude there was general agreement that we should continue on to Corfu Town itself.

We had a look around and decided to return another day and explore more fully.

Of course, having walked as far as Corfu Town, we then had to walk back. God, it was miles! We thought we were going for a pleasant stroll. Instead it was more of a route march! We yomped 5 miles there and – thanks to a short cut – just less than 5 miles back.

Needless to say, a brief siesta was called for prior to attending the poolside barbecue and buffet – accompanied by live music and Greek dancing – that evening.

The next day we went to visit the little church of the Virgin Mary on Pontkonissi (Mouse Island), only a stone's throw from our hotel. To get to the church there is a small, narrow jetty. Although intended for pedestrians, there were some airheads who felt the need to ride across on their motor bikes and frighten the life out of those walking, who had to jump out of their way.

I noted with some satisfaction that one of these riders had got his just desserts. About halfway along the jetty, there was a new-looking motor bike in the water being lashed by the waves.

On the way back, a huge 737 aircraft flew less than a hundred feet above our heads, having just taken off from the airport. We all got such a fright that we nearly ended up in the water ourselves!

Most of the holiday was spent sunbathing, walking or swimming (not me; I can't swim) whether in the sea, the indoor pool or the outdoor pool, depending on the weather.

One afternoon we went down to the beach and Dad put his towel on a large, flat rock so he would have somewhere to sit on the rare occasions he wasn't in the water. Jimmy sat in the shade, Mam and Katherine had sunbeds and I found another rock so I perched myself on it like the mermaid in the harbour at Copenhagen, except that I was dressed. I don't go in the water; I read.

Mam and Katherine went for a swim and all of a sudden, there was a commotion and they came hurrying out of the water. They had both been stung by a jelly fish, the same one apparently. Katherine's sting wasn't too bad; it must have just caught her between the thumb and forefinger.

Mam's sting looked really nasty and was evidently very painful. There were two long, angry-looking welts across her wrist. We went upstairs to find something with which to treat the stings but it was some time before she ventured back in the water. She had the marks on her wrist for months afterwards.

The following morning there was a veritable hurricane blowing so we couldn't go anywhere. We sat on our respective balconies reading books and watching the aircraft land or take off. In the afternoon the others went to the indoor pool and later that evening there was a very competitive game of ten pin bowling. I kept score.

By the time we went back upstairs, a huge electrical storm had started and it was pouring with rain. Of course, being English we aren't used to heavy rain so we sat on the balcony, drank coffee and watched the rain lashing down.

It was quite late when we decided to try and get some sleep and that proved quite difficult because the storm raged on for another couple of hours. Eventually it died away, only to resume at 5am! Fortunately, later that morning it was fresh, sunny and clear again.

Dad suggested that we should try to see some more of the island so we walked to the bus station to catch a bus to Paleokastritsa. This was said to be a very beautiful spot and we would no doubt see other nice places *en route*.

Well, there's a saying about the best laid plans, isn't there?

By the time we found the bus station and worked out which stand was ours, we'd missed the bus but several friendly locals assured us that another number 31 bus would arrive at one o'clock. We spent 50 minutes suffocating in the diesel-ridden bus station and by quarter past one when the bus still hadn't arrived, we were all feeling a bit frazzled.

We were debating whether or not to go back to the hotel and forget the whole thing, when we saw the bus to

Paleokastritsa pulling out. It was the number 13 not the number 31.

We went for a walk around Corfu Town instead.

Our attempt at exploring was much more successful the following day when we took a boat trip. It was very relaxing, very interesting and an absolute bargain at only 100 Drachma (about £3.50) each.

Our boatman pointed out all the places of interest, including the ancient port of Agamemnon and the fortress, the birthplace of the first Prime Minister of Greece (the building is now part of the University), the coast of Albania and the former convict island of Vigo, which I'd read about in Gerald Durrell's book.

On the top of the heavily wooded Analipsis Hill stands the villa of Mon Repos, said to be built on the ruins of the ancient city. The villa was built in 1826 by the British Commissioner for his wife, who was herself from Corfu.

Unfortunately, he was sent to serve in India shortly afterwards. It then became the summer residence of the Governors of Corfu and when King George 1 of Greece came to the throne, the British presented him with the villa.

Our own Prince Philip was born there in 1921.

Mon Repos is now a museum and its grounds are a public park surrounded by an ancient forest.

A couple of days before the end of the holiday, Dad and I decided we wanted to go to the shop near the little church on Pontikonissi so we went to the bank in the hotel to exchange some money first. The bank was supposed to open at 9am but it was still closed when we got there at 11am.

We returned half an hour later to find that the bank was still closed so – following the instructions in the hotel services directory – we went to the cashier's desk at reception to change our money there. The cashier evidently hadn't read the hotel services directory and was extremely reluctant to part with any cash. She said she didn't have any and told us we had to go to the nearest bank, which was in Corfu Town.

Now, I'm a very patient and tolerant person and I don't mind the little local quirks and customs when I'm abroad. I don't mind the general disregard for timetables, the random opening hours and the lack of the concept of time – although it has to be said that it does make it quite difficult for anyone trying to transact business – but when I'm confronted by someone who just wants to be awkward, I assume my best Margot Leadbetter persona.

I pointed out as calmly as I could that – according to the guest services directory, which the hotel had thoughtfully provided for the convenience of guests – the bank's opening hours were from 9am to 12.30pm, Monday to Friday, that today was Friday and the bank wasn't open.

I also advised her that according to said directory, when the bank is closed, the cashier will be "happy to help". Well, I can't say she was exactly happy as prescribed in the directory but in the end she decided she would part with some cash.

Katherine rounded off our last day with another little accident when she scalded her hand in the steam from the kettle. We plunged her hand into cold water and apart from being a bit red, it seemed fine.

After dinner on our last night, we sat on the balcony and had a drink whilst watching a particularly beautiful sunset. Once it got dark we could see the lights of Corfu Town in the distance and sometime later, the lights went out at the airport. That signalled that there would be no more flights that night so at least we knew we'd get a decent night's sleep.

It was also the last night for many of the staff, who were returning to their homes on the Greek mainland now that the season was over. They stood on the steps of the hotel and took photos before they dispersed, with promises to meet up the following season.

The next night, we flew home. Our aircraft picked up a bit of turbulence over Germany and it remained with us all the way back to Newcastle. Most people were asleep and unaware of it.

It was still dark and a bit chilly when we arrived at Newcastle Airport at 4.30 in the morning.

Did I find the Corfu of Gerald Durrell's childhood? Well, certainly some aspects of it: the little coves and bays, the olive groves and fruit trees, the beautiful scenery and the friendly and exuberant people…..it was all still there.

You have to carefully select where to go, of course but in spite of mass tourism, the essence of the real Corfu can still be found.

'Gradually the magic of the island settled over us as gently and clingingly as pollen'   (Gerald Durrell, 'My Family and Other Animals')

Mouse Island, Corfu

Action shots of Dad diving in the pool at the Hilton, Kanoni, Corfu

Chapter 3   Mauritius

'To travel is to live'   *(Hans Christian Andersen)*

In 2007 I celebrated my 50th birthday, so Jimmy and I decided to book a three week, all-inclusive holiday to Mauritius. I didn't know very much about Mauritius other than it was home to the now extinct Dodo, it was in the Indian Ocean and it was one of those places referred to as a 'paradise island' but that was enough.

However, my step-mother-in-law (who was in her 90's) hadn't been too well and was becoming increasingly confused so we thought it would be safer to go somewhere a bit closer to home in case anything happened. She died later that year, just after her 93rd birthday.

Our holiday to Mauritius finally took place in 2008 and was very 'long haul'. It was a bonus that we could travel from our local airport at Newcastle, albeit with a changeover at Dubai. Emirates Airlines had started what amounted to a shuttle service between Newcastle and Dubai so on the same aircraft we flew on, there were other passengers travelling to catch connecting flights to Indonesia, Thailand and Australia.

We left Newcastle around 1.45pm and after a pleasant and comfortable flight, we arrived in Dubai at midnight, local time. Our connecting flight to Mauritius was due to leave at 2.55am so we had some time to look around.

Dubai Airport is enormous; very modern, very crowded and pretty soulless but that's hardly surprising as it's predominantly a transit airport. The huge rectangular concourse is bright, spacious and full of shops, bars and cafes.

I was rather surprised to discover that in this vast and modern airport – and considering Dubai's emerging status as one of the world's leading financial and commercial hubs- I was unable to receive any kind of signal on my mobile phone.

Our onward flight to Mauritius took six hours and we arrived at 9.30am. There was quite a lengthy transfer to the hotel and we didn't arrive until midday. It had been a long and tiring journey (I can never sleep on an aircraft, no matter how tired I am) but we had three weeks to recover.

All the hotels in the area are on the beach but from what I saw, our hotel had the best location because the beach was at its widest at that point, whereas most hotels only had a fairly narrow stretch of beach in front. The beaches were all open; there were no sections cordoned off for specific hotels.

Mauritius is located 1,200 miles from the south east coast of Africa. Although it had been visited by the Arabs and the Portugese, the island had remained uninhabited until it became a Dutch colony in 1638. The Dutch named it 'Mauritius' after Prince Maurice von Nassau. They abandoned the colony in 1710 and in 1715, it became a French colony under the name 'Isle de France'.

When the French surrendered to the British at the end of the Napoleonic War in December 1810, the island once more reverted to its original name of Mauritius. Mauritius became an independent state in 1968 with a democratic system of government.

The population numbers around 1.26 million and although there is no 'official' language as such, the two main languages are English and French. Around 48.5% of the population are Hindu, 33% are Christian (mainly Catholic) and 17.3% are Muslim. There is also a small number of Buddhists.

Mauritius is multi-cultural, multi-ethnic, multi-lingual and multi-religious. Education is free and literacy rates are around 90%. I was surprised to learn that the 'O' and 'A' level exams are carried out by the University of Cambridge in the UK, through its international programme.

See; sometimes it's worth attending the meetings with the rep!

The island is still the only known habitat of the Dodo, a flightless bird which was hunted to extinction by human activity soon after the island was settled. Even so, the bird still appears on the Coat of Arms of Mauritius and on many souvenirs.

As I've already mentioned, Mauritius is known as a 'paradise island', along with a number of others across the globe. It has long, white, sandy beaches and clear blue water and the reef – which completely encircles the island – is one of the longest in the world. The island is also volcanic, which means there are spectacular views to be found.

Tropical rainstorms are a feature and whilst the rain can be torrential, the showers are usually short-lived. Just in case, the hotel thoughtfully provided an umbrella in each room so guests could walk between buildings, along the beach or further afield without getting wet.

The rooms were large and spacious, not luxuriously but comfortably – if sparsely - furnished. I have to say that the food was limited, not in quality but in choice. This can be a feature of many 'all inclusive' hotels.

One night the theme was an 'Indian Night', which in practice meant curry. Jimmy likes curry but I don't, so dinner that night was always going to be a challenge but I was sure there would be an alternative.

I was wrong.

There was chicken curry, lamb curry, beef curry, vegetable curry and even fish curry. I decided to try the soup because I thought I'd be safe with 'chicken mulligatawny'. I wasn't; it had curry powder in!

After dinner one night, we were sitting in the lounge having a drink. I had discovered one called 'Ti Punch'. It was a mixture of vodka, lemon juice, slivers of ice, tiny pieces of lemon and sugar cane juice and it was delicious.

I happened to look up to see a tall, elderly man walk in. I recognised him immediately. He had long, white hair, a white beard and he wore white Bermuda shorts and a white Hawaiian shirt with large black flowers printed on it. It was Santa!

I'd often wondered what he did in the summer. I was pleased to see that he was managing to have a break before the Christmas rush started.

I was wondering whether I should go over and try to get a head start on the Christmas lists, when the waiter came over with our drinks. He asked whether we would be staying for the entertainment. I asked what was on and he smiled and said "Games".

Jimmy and I looked at each other.

The waiter leaned forward as though about to impart a secret and said "Funny games". That was our cue to leave.

I have come to the conclusion that there are certain unwritten rules about being on holiday; certain things that people have to do. One of them is a trip on a glass-bottom boat (assuming you're anywhere near the sea, of course). Another is a visit to a local market.

Well, not being the sort of people who flout the rules, we did both.

We booked a taxi to take us to the market on the first Sunday after our arrival. It's the day that local people go so although we knew it would be busy, we thought it would be a good time to soak up some atmosphere.

There were dozens of fairly typical market stalls, each with canvas tops in case of a sudden downpour. Between the stalls on the left and right there was about an eighteen -inch gap so people could walk along the row. I say 'walk' but perhaps 'squeeze past each other' would be a more accurate description.

The stalls were piled high with pashminas, children's clothes, baby clothes, beautiful saris in every colour imaginable, hand-embroidered items from handkerchiefs to tablecloths, fake designer tee-shirts as well as endless varieties of fruit, vegetables and spices; in short, everything that any self-respecting market should have.

I bought two beautifully soft pashminas for 400 rupees and I have taken them with me on every holiday since then. The stall-holder gave me a small card which was imaginatively entitled 'The Pashmina Story'. It not only provided useful information on caring for my pashmina (for example; a pashmina should not be dry cleaned as the chemicals affect the softness) but also some fascinating facts.

Did you know, for instance, that the word 'pashmina' comes from the Persian word for 'wool', or that the wool itself comes from the undercoat of the Himalayan Mountain Goat, raised by semi-nomadic herders?

Well you know now.

The day we went on the glass-bottom boat, the sea was a bit choppy but as we were on the land side of the reef it wasn't as bad as the other side where the deep water was. We didn't see many fish but we had a very good view of the coral itself. The dominant variety seemed to be brown and twig-like, tipped with blue or purple.

On our return to shore, we went to the restaurant in search of some lunch, only to discover that the restaurant was empty. One of the staff told us that lunch was being served on the beach. We set off to find what the speciality of the day was.

It appeared to be flies.

The food had been set out on trestle tables covered with white cloths and there were several chaffing dishes in evidence but none of the food had been covered. Every fly within calling distance must have thought it was its birthday and they brought their family and friends along to join in the celebration.

Several guests raised concerns with the staff and it was clear that the kitchen and serving staff had more idea about food hygiene than the management. We spoke to one of the managers, who told us that they were trying this for the first time as an experiment. It wasn't clear whether the purpose of the experiment was to determine whether the guests preferred their lunch *'al fresco'* or whether it was to find the quickest way of spreading dysentery but whatever the reason, that was the last time that lunch was served on the beach.

Almost every day we would take a walk along the beach and back, about an hour and a half round trip. There was a point along the beach where it was possible to cut through to the nearby town of Belle Mare. One day we decided to go there for a change.

There were several designer shops which were said to be cheaper than other places but we didn't see any evidence of that. I saw a DKNY vest top priced at £65 and Gant and Hugo Boss polo shirts for £225 each.

In some of the shops we found the sales assistants a bit over-enthusiastic. Having been to Egypt on numerous occasions we were well used to the 'hard sell' but I don't think we expected to find it so prevalent here.

As we walked around the shops, two sales assistants were constantly at our shoulder. We only had to glance at something and it would be picked up, presented to us with a full description of what it was, its purpose and function and then we'd be shown what it looked like in artificial light in the shop and natural light outside. We knew everything but the price.

That's shopping the hard way and I don't like it. I know they're keen to make a sale but all that happens is that customers end up feeling pressured and they tend to leave the store without buying anything.

On the way back to the hotel that day, we were caught in a sudden and torrential shower and were forced to take shelter in a kind of summer house belonging to one of the other hotels. Two of the staff who had been on duty at the pool came over and gave us clean towels so we could dry off.

I should mention at this point that all the Mauritian people we came across were genuinely friendly and welcoming, very helpful and endlessly cheerful.

As an example, on hearing that I was having problems with my mobile phone, our taxi driver said he would sort something out for me by the time he took us on our next day trip a couple of days later. True to his word, he brought me a SIM card for the local provider (Emtel) which he'd taken from his wife's spare mobile phone.

She let me borrow it for the remainder of the holiday and I discovered I was only paying 2p per text! When I returned the SIM card at the end of the holiday I gave the taxi driver's wife a 'top up' voucher for $10. At 2p per text she's probably still using it!

Our taxi driver took us on a tour of the north part of the island and we spent an hour at the island's capital, Port Louis. It's an attractive harbour area with lots of bars, cafés, shops and restaurants and being the capital, lots of office blocks, too.

When we left the Port Louis, we went to visit the beautiful botanical gardens. They're known locally as the Jardin Botanique Sir Seewoosagur Ramgoolan, which is why tourists refer to them as 'the botanical gardens'.

Sir Seewoosagur Ramgoolan was the first Prime Minister of Mauritius after independence in 1968 and is called 'the father of the nation'. His funerary monument can be seen in the gardens.

The gardens are beautiful, with wide, tree-lined avenues – particularly the impressive avenue of Royal Palms – as well as large pools containing Asian lotus plants (mainly white and yellow) or giant lily pads with frogs and tadpoles. Also worth a look is the enclosure of giant tortoises, for which the island is famous.

We spent a pleasant and relaxing couple of hours there and it was worth taking the time out to visit.

A couple of days later – it was the end of our second week – we went into the hotel restaurant to have lunch and the manager told us that our 'all-inclusive' package was finished. I said no, we still had another week to go. He showed me his paperwork and sure enough, it contained our name and room number, room 249, and stated 'Bed and breakfast from 9th to 16th June.'

Knowing I was right but wondering what had gone wrong, I went back to the room to retrieve our paperwork. I took it back to reception and after a bit of paper-shuffling, they admitted they had made a mistake and they apologised. How many people do that these days? They duly amended their records and we continued to enjoy our 'all-inclusive' for a further week.

Our final visit of the holiday was to the south west part of the island, which is said to be the most picturesque. As we drove along, the scenery changed from fields of pineapples, carrots, cabbages and potatoes to plantations of tobacco, tea, coffee and sugar cane. Mauritius is home to the second largest sugar refinery in the world.

There were rows of coconut palms and Banyan trees with Morning Glory wound around the trunks and yet in some places, the scenery reminded me very much of the English countryside.

I hadn't realised that Mauritians drive on the left and they even have traffic lights, speed bumps and roundabouts; another legacy of British colonial rule! Most of the cars however, are Japanese.

I mentioned earlier that Mauritius as an island is multi-religious; in fact, freedom of religion is enshrined in the island's constitution. In one small area we saw a mosque, a Tamil temple, a Buddhist shrine and a Catholic church within a few hundred yards of each other.

One of the most impressive places we visited was the Temple on the Lake, a peaceful, tranquil Buddhist site. It was beautiful and must have looked stunning when the sun was shining.

Unfortunately, it was raining heavily when we arrived but that created a haze over the lake, which was very atmospheric.

Near the entrance to the site there is a giant statue of the god Shiva. It stands 109 feet high and is made of stone but it has been so highly polished that it looks like bronze.

On the way to the next location, the taxi driver stopped to pick some fruit for his family from the various trees which grew along the roadside.

Our journey took us to the picturesque Black River Gorge National Park. There is one particular vantage point with spectacular views over the Gorge itself and a beautiful waterfall to the right hand side. I love spectacular views; waterfalls, mountains, volcanoes, valleys. I wasn't disappointed here.

A visit to the volcano known as the Kanaka Crater was an impressive reminder that the island was created during the Pliocene Period, about 10 million years ago. Technically this volcano is considered as 'dormant' and not 'dead' so it is possible that it could erupt again, although there is no sign that it has done so for hundreds if not thousands of years.

The final stop on the tour was a place called Chamarel, which is famous for the 'terre de sept couleurs' or the 'seven-coloured earth'. This anomaly is common to only a very small number of volcanic sites worldwide and I understand that something of the same can be seen on one of the Canary Islands.

There is a walkway around the site where the coloured earth is exposed to get a better view of all the colours. It is quite an amazing sight and the colours seem to become lighter or darker depending on the weather and the angle from which they're viewed.

Nearby is the Cascade Chamarel, another lovely waterfall in a smaller but very pretty gorge and on the way out, another enclosure of giant tortoises. All these lovely things can be seen at Chamarel for an amazing 75 Rupees admission charge. Bargain.

On our last day on Mauritius, we were able to stay in the hotel room for an extra couple of hours but we still had a 5 hour wait in reception before the mini bus came to take us to the airport. The waiters twice brought us coffee during that time and they didn't charge us for it, so that was very much appreciated. We were also given a voucher for lunch as this time, our 'all inclusive' package really had expired at noon that day!

The mini bus came for us at 8pm and we had an hour's drive to pick up two more people before travelling on to the airport. It was quite a scary ride; hairpin bends, driving at speed, no streetlights and our unsecured suitcases (which had been placed on the back seat) sliding all over the place.

On arrival at the airport, there was no-one to show us where to go or what to do but we figured it out for ourselves and before too long, we had embarked on the first leg of our homeward journey from Mauritius to Dubai. The flight took six and a half hours and just before we came in to land, we witnessed a beautiful sunrise.

So vast is the airport at Dubai that we only had half an hour to get from one end of the concourse to the other, go through the usual security checks and get to our gate. It was a bit of a rush but we made it.

I was really tired and therefore, convinced I would sleep once we were airborne. Well, that didn't happen. It was freezing on the aircraft and everyone spent the journey huddled in blankets. In addition, we endured the longest continuous bout of turbulence I've ever experienced. It wasn't just the occasional shudder; it was lots of shudders and bumps and every so often, a stomach-churning plunge of a hundred feet or more. It made those of us who were still awake feel very nervous and of course, made the journey seem endless.

Actually, the journey only took a little over seven hours but by the time we had arrived at Newcastle I wasn't even sure what day it was. I didn't care really; it was just a relief to be back on *'terra firma'*.

Once again, we had seen some amazing sights and experienced the friendliness of the local people. It had seemed a long time to spend on an island and on a beach holiday and I suppose it would have been easy to spend the whole three weeks sunbathing, which I know some people do.

Personally, I can't see the point in paying what amounts to quite a lot of money to go somewhere and just lie on a beach or by a pool all day. What is the point of travelling if you aren't going to experience a new place, new sights, some of the history and culture? Isn't that what travel is supposed to be about?

You can still lie by the pool when you come back from a visit, between visits or at the beginning or end of a holiday but there's more to a holiday than getting a sun tan. After all,

'The sand may brush off, the salt may wash away, the tans may fade but the memories will last forever'
(Anonymous)

The harbour at Port Louis, Mauritius

The Temple on the Lake.

Statue of the god, Shiva, Temple on the Lake

Sunset at the beach, Mauritius

Botanical gardens, Mauritius

The seven-coloured earth at Chamarel

Chapter 4   Bali

'We live in a wonderful world that is full of beauty, charm and adventure'   *('The Blonde Abroad')*

I don't know where the idea came from to go to Bali in 2002. It hadn't been a long-standing ambition and I don't recall it featuring in earlier conversations about holidays but for some reason, we decided to go that year.

We had made a conscious decision many years earlier that when we were choosing holidays destinations, we would try and visit the long haul ones first and leave the nearer ones until later. One reason was that in those days, it was possible to get some exceptionally good deals, particularly on long haul and another was that the age difference between Jimmy and me (16 years) meant that we didn't know how long 'far off' destinations would be an option.

We had also come across so many people who had told us that they wished they had visited some place or other whilst their partner was still alive or whilst they themselves were still fit enough to travel. It's no good waiting until it's too late.

'If you are planning that trip of a lifetime, longing to see the world, don't let things delay or stop you. For me, the number one reason for travel is that you may not get the chance again.'   *(The Guy, 'Flights and Frustrations')*

One of the biggest Issues - and a particular bugbear of mine - is the outrageous premiums that insurance companies charge travellers, based only on their age. Age Discrimination legislation appears not to apply to insurance companies……..but don't get me started on that!

Whatever the reason, Bali was our chosen destination in 2002. I didn't know very much about the island before we booked, only that it sounded very exotic and was said to be very beautiful. The added bonus was that if we booked in January, we would be given a free upgrade to an executive room.

Like our visit to Mauritius, travelling to Bali involved several changes of aircraft and an extremely long journey. I suppose that's why it's called 'long haul'.

We left Newcastle Airport at 6.30am on October 3rd to fly to Heathrow. Our connecting flight to Kuala Lumpur was due to leave at noon and although it was a British Airways holiday, we were flying on Malaysian Airlines. We were due to reach Kuala Lumpur at 7.30am the following day and would be leaving there at 9.50am for the final leg of the journey to Denpasar Airport on Bali.

We were due to land at Denpasar at 12.50pm. The time difference is GMT + 7 hours.

Fortunately, all our flights were on schedule and we had no problems getting there.

I have to say that the food on the Malaysian Airlines flight was excellent on both the outward and inbound journeys. According to the menus – which I made a note of – lunch consisted of:

Coronation chicken salad, bread roll

Grilled, herbed cod with lemon and honey sauce, potatoes, carrots and broccoli
Winter berry cake with raspberry coulis
Ice cream

Breakfast the following morning consisted of:

Chilled orange juice
Yoghurt with fresh fruit salad
Mushroom omelette, hash brown, chicken sausage, grilled tomato
Croissant with butter and jam

Our route from London Heathrow to Kuala Lumpur took us over Dover, Belgium, Austria, Germany, across the southern part of Russia, over Afghanistan and Iran and then over India, just south of Jaipur. I suspect I would feel a lot less comfortable flying over some of those places now.

The airport at Kuala Lumpur is large, modern, spacious and bright. It felt welcoming and not as impersonal as some others we've been through. We had a two hour wait for our connecting flight which then took another two hours to get to Bali.

I was very impressed with the airport at Denpasar, too. It was a simple, traditional-looking yet modern building and again, it felt welcoming. It even had a small replica temple inside.

There was a large notice at the entrance to the arrivals hall which – whilst not what you could call 'welcoming' - was certainly very clear. It was in several languages and had a large sealed bin on either side. It said in essence, that if passengers were carrying drugs of any sort or quantity, they should place them in the bins provided and no further action would be taken.

It then went on to warn passengers that once they had passed that point and entered the airport building, should they be found to be carrying drugs they would be arrested. Bali has the death penalty for those trafficking or smuggling drugs.

Well I thought that was fair warning; clear and unequivocal.

I get really annoyed when people who are all too well aware of the penalties, choose to smuggle drugs and then whine when they get caught that their punishment is too harsh. All the 'do-gooders' come out of the woodwork and complain that it isn't fair that the smuggler should be subject to the laws of the country in which they committed their crime.

Our transit from the airport at Denpasar to the Melia Benoa Hotel at Tanjung Benoa, took about twenty minutes. The hotel is close to the tourist district of Nusa Dua in the south of the island.

The hotel and grounds were stunning. There were no doors on the hotel itself and the public areas were 'open plan' in order to allow the breeze to blow through as the area is very humid. There were plants and greenery everywhere, together with Balinese statues.

There were countless little details all over the hotel and grounds which added to the ambiance: stone fonts filled with water and flower petals, patterns drawn in the sand which surrounded the little indoor garden features and even marigold heads in the sand-filled ash trays in the public areas.

Our room overlooked the lush, tropical gardens which were full of palm trees, plants and flowers and there was a lovely water feature. Through the trees to the right of our balcony, was the swimming pool and beyond that was the narrow path which led to the beach.

We had been shown to our lovely room by a very affable member of staff who pointed out all its features together with the beautiful view and he seemed even more excited than we were!

After having made sure that we were ecstatic with our room he left us to unpack. It was a day or two before we discovered that the room – lovely and comfortable though it was – was not the one we had been promised. It was a standard room. I should say that we were happy with it; it was large and spacious, comfortable, clean and attractively furnished but it was not an executive room and that's what we'd booked.

We raised this with Guest Services and later, with British Airways Holidays, where we were advised to lodge an official complaint. British Airways in turn, took it up with the hotel and a couple of weeks after we arrived home, we had a telephone call from our travel agent, Dawson and Sanderson. They told us that they had a refund cheque for £750 for us, this being the difference between the cost of the room we had and the one we should have had.

The sandy beach was cleared of seaweed several times a day and as Bali is surrounded by coral reefs, the coastal waters are calm and shallow. The tide goes out quite a long way, leaving rock pools and sand banks.

There are about 500 different species of marine life on and around the reef, including rays and turtles. There are also sea snakes, reef sharks and hammerhead sharks.

The sand on the south of the island is white, whereas in the north and west it is black and volcanic. The region itself is still highly volcanic and as recently as November 2015, flights in and out of Denpasar were suspended and travellers temporarily stranded when clouds of volcanic ash began spewing from Mount Rinjani on the nearby island of Lombok. The winds blew the ash towards Bali for several days and whilst there was no danger to the population from the volcano itself, obviously aircraft can't fly through ash clouds.

The last serious volcanic activity on Bali occurred in 1962, when Mount Agung erupted killing thousands of people and having a devastating effect on the economy.

We had arrived on Bali at the start of the monsoon season, which runs from October to April but that doesn't mean it rains all the time. In fact, the weather during our stay was mostly dry, although it was very humid most of the time.

A couple of days into the holiday, we went in for breakfast as usual to discover that the chef was having some difficulty lighting the gas- powered grill. Suddenly, the thing blew back and exploded quite violently. Had the chef been standing any nearer he would have been badly hurt. As it was, I think he just got a bit singed.

Two maintenance men appeared and tried to fix the grill but eventually they gave up and took it away.

No eggs for breakfast that morning.

One of the considerations for potential travellers thinking about booking a holiday to Bali is that during Balinese New Year (Nyepi – the day of the spirits) there is a 24-hour period of silence observed. This lasts from 6am one day to 6am the next and during this time there is no work, travel or entertainment and the airport is closed.

Actual dates vary each year so it is best to check in advance. In 2013, Nyepi took place on March 13th, in 2014 it was March 31st, in March 2015 it was March 21st and in 2016, March 9th.

There are several customs and social codes to observe on Bali so as not to cause offence:

Do not show the soles of your feet or shoes,

Do not touch anyone on the head, especially children

Do not point or beckon with your finger

Do not stand with your hands on your hips

When eating or passing around food or gifts, use only your right hand

Cover your head, legs and shoulders when visiting temples and mosques

It is considered polite to shake hands on meeting or parting

Balinese people are soft-spoken, courteous, polite and friendly. They are also very religious. Of the population of around 4.2 million, 83.5% are Balinese Hindu, 13.4% are Muslim, 2.5% are Christian and 0.5% are Buddhist.

The island is 69 miles north to south and 95 miles east to west and there is evidence of human habitation going back to 2,000 BC.

The first European contact was with the Portugese in 1512 (there are very few places in the world that the Portugese didn't reach first!) although they didn't settle there. Following the arrival of the Dutch explorer Cornelius de Hautman in 1597, the Dutch East India Company was established on Bali in 1602.

The Japanese occupied Bali during the Second World War and their presence was resented more than that of the Dutch. Bali was finally granted independence on 29th December 1949.

One day we went to visit the nearby shopping centre of Galleria Nusa Dua, only about twenty minutes' walk from our hotel. The area is very quiet with hardly any traffic. It is beautifully maintained with flowers, plants, trees and tiny temples and shrines on the roundabouts. The road itself is tree-lined, as are the long drives which lead up to various 4 and 5 star hotels (including the Sheraton and Hilton) set well back from the road.

As we walked along, we were approached by a young man on a motor cycle and in spite of his assurances that he wasn't selling anything, we knew he hadn't just stopped us to say "Hello". We decided to play along for a while. He presented us with a 'scratch card' each and when the numbers were revealed, guess what? We had both won a prize!

I had won a t-shirt but miraculously, Jimmy had won 10,000 US dollars! Who'd have thought? Especially as we hadn't paid for the 'scratch cards'! To collect our prizes, all we had to do was to go to a nearby hotel by taxi (which the young man could arrange for us) and we would soon receive the money.

Unfortunately, we felt unable to accept his kind offer, although I must admit, the decision was made easier knowing it was a scam.

There was no 10,000 US dollar prize; the whole thing was an elaborate charade to sell timeshare!

We arrived at the very modern Galleria Nusa Dua where we found a number of traditional market stalls selling pottery and ceramics, wood carvings and incense. There were also a number of designer stores, including Benetton and Moschino and a single storey department store, which was a veritable Aladdin's cave. It sold everything from cosmetics and clothes to household items, books and souvenirs; a sort of Indonesian House of Fraser.

Once inside the store, we were approached by a young lady who according to her name badge, was called 'Trainee'. She proceeded to ask us some questions from a list on the clipboard she was carrying. They seemed innocuous enough but there didn't seem any pattern or purpose to them. We began to suspect another scam, especially when 'Trainee' told us that our details would be entered into a prize draw and if we won, we would be contacted at our hotel.

Well, in another freakish coincidence, we were indeed contacted at our hotel later that day and advised that we had won first prize! How lucky were we?

Our prize was a voucher; a voucher for us to stay at a hotel for eight days and seven nights and which would be valid for two years. All we had to do was to return to the store within two days and the whole process would take about an hour and a half. Clearly, it was yet another timeshare scam.

The following day we went on a tour called 'The Natural Beauty of Bali', although the first few visits were to shops. The area is called 'Obud' and it is almost exclusively populated by artisans.

The first stop was at a silversmith's shop and after a minute or two of being shown how to convert silver into silver thread (which is 93% silver and 7% copper), we were ushered inside to look at the many and varied goods on sale. They seemed rather expensive but I did buy a couple of items; a bracelet for Katherine and a filigree brooch for Mam. They cost me a total of 31 US dollars.

The next stop was at a woodcraft co-operative and again, there were some lovely items on display, from large statues to small trinket boxes and there was a lot of very ornate work. I paid 6 US dollars for a very nice wooden Buddha with a very smiley face.

The final stop at Obud was at an art gallery where there was a large range of oil, watercolour and charcoal pictures available. I didn't buy anything there; we had no wall space left at home to hang any more art.

Our journey took us through some magnificent scenery, including a great many rice terraces surrounded by banana plants and coconut palms. There are temples and shrines everywhere – there's a good reason why Bali is referred to as 'the island of 1000 temples' – and local people make offerings of food, incense or flowers every day. Religion plays a significant role in the everyday lives of Balinese people.

I had picked up a flower as we were walking around and placed it on a small shrine. The policeman nearby thanked me.

We stopped for an hour at a restaurant on top of a hill and the view was spectacular; green hills, well-manicured gardens, forests and rice fields as far as the eye could see. Farmers on Bali practice rotation farming (one of the few things I remembered from my school geography lessons all those years ago) and rice accounts for two of the three crops farmers grow every year.

We visited the impressive Temple of Ulun Danu on the shores of Lake Bratan, the so-called 'Temple on the Lake', where we could walk around the whole site but not actually enter the remains of the temple itself. It certainly has a magnificent setting, with its tree-covered hills shrouded in mist as well as the dark waters of the lake itself.

As we drove up into the hills, the coach stopped so we could get out and see some of the monkeys that live in the area. We bought some nuts with which to feed them and some were more willing to accept food than others. The group nearest to us was a family group; a large male, several females and a number of babies and juveniles.

There are two species of monkey on Bali; the Crab-eating Monkey and the Macaque. The latter is mainly to be found around temples and close to human habitation, presumably because it is easier to find food.

We had a pleasant day exploring some of the scenic places for which Bali is famous and a couple of days later, we booked a taxi to go on another tour, this time to see the still active volcano at Batur.

The views of the volcano and the nearby outcrop of volcanic rock known as the Cone of Batur, were amazing. The volcano is mildly explosive with occasional ejections of lave. The nearby lake – or caldera – was equally beautiful, with its milky blue-green waters surrounded by dark green vegetation. A very picturesque spot indeed.

On the way back to the hotel, we drove through a plantation area where there were many different types of plants growing. They included pineapple, vanilla, coffee, tea, cocoa, mango and snake fruit (so called because if its peculiar skin).

The waters around Bali are clear and teeming with a large variety of marine life. Jimmy used to go snorkelling until the day someone asked him whether he was afraid of the sharks? Sharks? That was the end of the snorkelling!

We took a boat trip, which provided us with a great opportunity to see many of the fish that swam on or around the reef. In particular, there were a lot of little blue and yellow ones, which we were told, were called 'Clown Fish'.

As we ventured further out on the boat, the sea became more and more choppy and as we turned to go against the direction of the waves, hitting them head on, it became even worse. The reason we were venturing out so far was to see dolphins or I wouldn't have risked it. I hate the water.

Suddenly, there they were! Lots of dolphins! Sometimes they were difficult to see amongst the waves but they would leap out of the water and buzz the prow of the boat or do somersaults or backflips as though in the sheer joy of being alive. We must have spent at least half an hour watching them twisting and turning, leaping and swimming. They're such beautiful creatures and they really seem to enjoy human contact. They always look as though they're smiling.

I could have stayed there much longer but the weather was changing and we needed to return to shore.

On the way back we called in briefly at Turtle Island. The boat had to drop us off about twenty yards from the shore as the water was very shallow and it couldn't get any nearer. We clambered over the side of the boat and walked calf-deep in clear blue, very warm water to the shore.

Apart from the usual enclosure of turtles, there was also a python, a couple of monkeys, a toucan, a giant bat and a hawk. It was soon apparent that this was a photo opportunity place. One of the staff placed the toucan on my arm and it scratched me. I don't think it meant to; it was just trying to get a firmer grip.

Luckily the scratch didn't break the skin and I knew my tetanus shots were up to date so I wasn't too concerned.

Next, someone produced the biggest bat I'd ever seen and draped it over my wrist. The bat didn't seem to mind. I quite like bats but I'd always thought they were tiny things, a bit like mice with wings. This monstrous creature hung there upside down and I soon discovered that it was as heavy as it was large. My arm began to ache and when I tried to lift it, the bat extended its wings, as bats do. It was like carrying a large, black umbrella!

Apparently it was a fruit bat and their wing span can be as much as five and a half feet. They can also weigh up to three and a half pounds. The one I had certainly did!

The following day – Sunday October 13th – started like any other day but it didn't remain so for long.

We were coming back upstairs from breakfast and as we arrived in the lobby, we met a lady that we had spoken to a few times. I asked her if she was going out and she replied "Yes, if it's still on". I asked why it wouldn't be and she said "Haven't you heard the news this morning? A bomb exploded in a nightclub near here last night. A lot of people have been killed".

Apparently it had been on the news in the UK late the night before and the lady's daughter had been sending her text messages but because of the time difference, she hadn't picked them up until the next morning. We went straight to our room and switched on the television to hear the latest news.

The BBC was reporting that a bomb had been hidden inside a car and had exploded outside a nightclub in Kuta, a popular tourist area on Bali. As well as the nightclub, other properties and a number of cars had been damaged but worst of all, there were reports that at least 50 people – mostly Australians – had been killed.

An Australian Minister was saying that specially chartered aircraft were being sent to evacuate the remaining Australians from Bali.

The news reports and pictures were horrific and it suddenly occurred to me that if we were watching them on the BBC, these reports would also be shown back in the UK. I decided I had to phone and let the family know we were okay but then realised it was about 2am at home so I would have to wait.

All that day, people were talking in hushed voices about what had happened. Everyone was shocked and couldn't understand how such a thing could have happened in a place like Bali. Bad enough anywhere but why Bali? Nevertheless, everyone was resolute; this was an inhuman, inexcusable act perpetrated by barbarians against innocent people and it would have a devastating effect on Bali's tourist industry but none of us were going to let it ruin our holiday. We couldn't let these monsters win.

I heard variations on that theme many times.

As soon as it was a reasonable time at home, I tried to phone my parents. There was no answer and then I remembered that my sister and her family were moving house and my parents had gone to help them. I decided to phone Katherine in the hope she would be able to get a message to them. I knew she wouldn't be out of bed at that time on a Sunday morning but I didn't want her to hear the news from someone else, or worse still, from the television.

The conversation went something like this:

Me: Hello Katherine; it's me.
Katherine: Me who?
Me: It's your mother. I haven't been away that long.
Katherine: Where are you?
Me: Still in Bali but I thought I should ring you because of the news reports.
Katherine: What news reports?

Well, at £1 a minute I didn't think we were making much progress so I told her that there had been an explosion here on Bali and a lot of people had been killed but not to worry; we were fine. I told her to try and get in touch with her Gran and Granda and let them know that we were safe. It was obvious that she didn't know about the bombings at that point and had no idea what I was talking about but I knew she'd hear about it at some point so at least she wouldn't worry.

During the day the hotel management rang our room to check on us and later, there was a note pushed under our door which outlined what had happened, or at least, what was known at that point. The note stated that security had been increased and gave us numbers to contact for further information. It also confirmed that all the guests in our hotel were safe and accounted for.

British Airways also contacted us to make sure we were okay and to say that although there were no plans to evacuate travellers, if we wanted to leave they would get us home. It was reassuring but we didn't want to leave; after all, the deed had been done and whoever the perpetrators were, they'd probably be long gone.

It transpired that there had been explosions at two different locations at about 11pm the previous evening. One was at a place called Julan Niti Mandala, which is at Denpasar and there were no reports of injuries or fatalities there.

The greater catastrophe was at the Sari Nightclub at Kuta, in the north of the island. By midday we had heard reports of 100 dead and 120 injured and by that night, 158 people had been confirmed dead.

I have to say that we were appalled by the hyped-up, sensationalist and wholly inaccurate reporting by CNN during this time. It was the worst kind of journalism. According to CNN, holidaymakers were leaving the island in droves and there was widespread panic as tourists jammed the airport, desperate to catch a flight home.

It was disgusting and totally untrue. There was no panic at all (other than at CNN where they were clearly desperate to make the story last all day) and the majority of tourists were quite content to stay and complete their holiday. CNN had used some stock footage of a queue at Denpasar Airport to illustrate the 'crowds' trying to leave. Such a queue was normal at this airport, especially when there were two flights checking in at the same time; the end of the queue is often outside the airport doors for a short time.

CNN had taken a tragic event and manipulated and distorted it to create a drama. It showed a total lack of respect for the injured and deceased, for their families at home and for those of us still there. It also showed utter contempt for the efforts of the authorities who were working hard to deal with the situation.

We received another update from British Airways later that day, advising that their representatives were checking on the welfare of all their passengers. They also advised that flights from the UK to Bali had been suspended so by the time we were due to go home, there would hardly be anyone left. We were also told that the Foreign Office had updated their advice for travellers *viz:*

'We advise against al travel to Bali and against all holiday and non-essential travel to Indonesia at present'.

It was like a scene from 'Yes, Prime Minister'. It was all very well for the Foreign Office to issue advice to people at home but it wasn't much use to those of us already there! I don't know why British Airways felt the need to draw it to our attention.

We felt very sad for the Balinese people who were completely bewildered as to why anyone would do this. We spoke to our taxi driver, who was very upset as he was from Kuta and he said that he hoped the rest of the world would help Bali because they had no experience of dealing with anything like this.

Jimmy and I walked down to the beach at about 4.30 on that Sunday and watched the sunset. Sitting there listening to the birds singing, the sea lapping against the shore and the breakers crashing against the reef a few hundred yards away, it all seemed so peaceful. It was almost impossible to believe that such a terrible event could have occurred in such a beautiful and tranquil place.

At 1.30 in the morning, Katherine phoned to say that she had been watching the news reports (fortunately not CNN) and she just wanted to reassure herself that we were safe and well. She said people (friends, work colleagues, family members) had been telephoning her all day to see if she had heard anything. Katherine told us that 33 British tourists were amongst the dead and a young man from Durham was unaccounted for.

A couple of friends had telephoned our local branch of Dawson and Sanderson to ask if they had any news about us. Staff at Dawson and Sanderson rang the hotel to ask about us (which was very kind of them) and the hotel was able to tell them that we were safe; she had seen us go in for breakfast that morning.

A couple of days later, the Indonesian authorities announced that they wanted all tourists out of the country by the weekend. This meant that people who had only been there a day or two had to leave early but fortunately for us, our holiday would be over by then anyway.

On the afternoon of October 16th, we went for a walk along the beach and discovered that local people were planting little crosses in the sand, one for every person killed in the bombing. They also added garlands and other offerings to each cross. It was very moving.

The final death toll in this tragedy was 202.

The following day we went on another day trip with our taxi driver, this time to see the magnificent temple of Tanalot and a waterfall with the unlikely name of Git Git.

It was a three- hour drive to the north of the island and near Denpasar there was a build -up of traffic. Turning down one road we came across a very lengthy tailback. Eventually, our driver did a 'U' turn and took a different route. I asked if there had been an accident and he said "No; that's the road to Kuta".

Our journey took us through a lot of small villages, past rice fields and along the route we had taken a few days earlier when we had visited Ulun Danu. We passed the area where we had stopped to feed the monkeys and continued up the hill around some tight, hairpin bends then came down the other side.

We arrived at a roadside stop and our driver pointed the way to the waterfall. There was only one way in and out and it was along a path with sets of steps here and there. It wasn't too difficult walking down but I knew we'd suffer on the way back up. There were some market stalls selling souvenirs and local produce and there were a few seats to rest on.

Eventually, we reached the bottom of the steps and there was a shelter with seats right next to the stream which came from the waterfall. We sat in this shelter – which was basically six pillars holding up a roof; there were no sides. We ate our picnic lunch then walked a few steps to the site of the waterfall itself. I was quite surprised to find that the water was only a few inches deep, although nearer the fall it was a bit deeper but not by much.

The cliff and the waterfall were about a hundred feet high and there were quite a few rocks in the shallows to sit on. The whole setting was stunning; I could have stayed there all day, it was so peaceful and quiet.

Unfortunately, all too soon we had to endure the torturous climb back up to the entrance. There were zig-zag paths with flights of steps every few yards and climbing them in the humid heat of the afternoon was quite an ordeal. We stopped for a cold drink about halfway up but it didn't seem to help much. Eventually – and much the worse for wear – we reached the top and found our taxi driver waiting in the car park.

We set off on the return journey up the hill, past the monkeys, down the hill and past the 'temple on the lake', heading for the seaside. We found ourselves in a car park in front of an area that looked like a huge park with stalls and shops and we headed down to the sea. We had to climb down more steps then up a couple of flights of steps before we reached the magnificent coastal temple of Tanalot.

It was worth the climb, the location being superb. The temple is located on a small promontory above the Indian Ocean with the waves crashing all around. It was very impressive, although there was restoration work going on at the temple and there was scaffolding and a crane on a track behind it which spoilt the effect a little. Nevertheless, there were many different vantage points from which to enjoy the view.

There was another long and tiring climb back up to the car park but not as bad as the one at Git Git and then we had an hour's journey back to the hotel.

I was really glad we had taken the opportunity to explore something of the island, not only because of its beauty but because we realised it might be some time before tourists would be able to visit Bali again. It had lived up to all my expectations of what a 'paradise island' should be. There's a lot to see and to appreciate on Bali and I would certainly recommend it.

The following day we began the long journey home, leaving the hotel at 4.15 in the afternoon. Our flight to Kuala Lumpur was at 6.45 pm and as we walked through the departure lounge at Denpasar airport, we saw a dark red light shining through a window. Bali had laid on a spectacular sunset for us.

We left Kuala Lumpur at 11.40pm, heading for Heathrow and just as the aircraft doors were closing, a young man hurried on to the aircraft. He was casually dressed without a jacket or coat and he had no hand luggage. He sat in the only available seat, which was next to me. He had a meal during the flight but every time the stewardess came along with a tray of water, orange juice and tins of beer, he took one of the beers and gave it to us. We could never have drunk all that even if I had been a beer drinker!

The menu for the return flight was similar to the outbound one:

Dinner:

Curried chicken and potato salad with a bread roll
Beef curry with rice
White chocolate and banana slice

Of course, there was tea and coffee and pre-dinner drinks, too.

Breakfast the following morning consisted of:

Chilled orange juice
Smoothie yoghurt drink
Fresh fruit salad
Tomato & onion omelette, rosti potatoes, chicken sausage, button mushrooms
Croissant with butter and jam

Once the announcement had been made that we were about to start our decent into Heathrow Airport, our quiet companion unfastened his seatbelt and went to the rear of the aircraft. He didn't come back and no-one questioned where he was. We assumed he must have been a security person, which would explain his last minute boarding, lack of luggage and sudden disappearance.

It made us feel a little uneasy though. Sometimes increased security has the opposite effect to what's intended.

We arrived at Heathrow at 5.50 in the morning on 19th October and caught our flight up to Newcastle at 9.20. It was something of a relief to land safely back in Newcastle. It was a bright, cold and sunny day, although we weren't too sure at that point what day it was. It took several days to get back into a normal sleep pattern but was it worth it? Absolutely!

Bali is beautiful and its people are friendly but in a quiet and respectful way. The 2002 bombing did tremendous damage to the tourist industry but there have been signs that visitor numbers have been increasing in recent years. In 2010, there were 2.57 million tourists to Bali and this had risen to 2.88 million by 2012.

I saw a poster recently that read: *'Promise yourself that one day you'll wake up in Bali'*.

Sounded like good advice to me!

Temple of Ulun Danu on Lake Bratan

Cone of Batur and the caldera

Git Git waterfall

Chapter 5   Gibraltar

'A great way to learn about your country is to leave it'.
(Henry Rollins)

I should say straight away that we've never actually had a holiday in Gibraltar. "Why then..." I hear you ask – "...would you write a chapter about it?". Well, since you ask, I'll tell you.

I'd wanted to go to Gibraltar for a long time and when we were in Torremolinos, there was the option of a day trip so we decided to go. Why a separate chapter? Well, Gibraltar is such an interesting place that it deserves a chapter to itself and in any case, it really doesn't sit well in a chapter about Spain.

Sovereignty over Gibraltar is still a bone of contention between the Spanish and the British, in spite of two referenda (one in 1967 and one in 2002) which declared the overwhelming wish of its citizens to remain under British rule. In fact, in the 2002 referendum, 98% of Gibraltarians voted in favour of retaining British sovereignty.

The Royal Gibraltar Regiment army garrison and the Royal Navy squadron make up British Forces Gibraltar, which has its headquarters at the former RAF station on the island, although there are no longer any aircraft permanently stationed there.

In 2004, the Royal Naval base was granted the Freedom of the City of Gibraltar.

Gibraltar has the status of a 'British Overseas Territory' and was joined to Britain in 1713. Its 32,000 people have British citizenship. The population consists of 83.2% Gibraltarians, 9.5% 'other British', 3.5% Moroccan, 1.2% Spanish and 1% from other parts of the EU. 72% of the population is Catholic and the oldest church is the Cathedral of St Mary the Crowned, which dates from 1462.

Perhaps not surprisingly, the official language is English, although many people are bilingual, with Spanish being the other language.

Gibraltar shows evidence of Neanderthal habitation between 28,000 BC and 24,000 BC, although the name 'Gibraltar' dates from the Middle Ages when the Moors settled there. It originates from the Arabic term 'Jebel Tariq' ('the mountain of Tariq'). The 'mountain' referred to is the 1398 feet high, Jurassic limestone cliff commonly known as the 'Rock of Gibraltar'. It was formed after a shift in the tectonic plates about 150 million years ago.

Our brief visit to Gibraltar began at 9.15 am on Friday March 14th 2014 when a coach collected us from our hotel in Torremolinos. As well as a group of British tourists, there was also a sizeable group of Germans on the coach but our guide was fluent in both languages and could switch from one to the other and back again in a second.

She would give us the commentary in English and then repeat it in German. She must have been exhausted by the end of the day!

Our route took us from Torremolinos and Benalmadena to Fuengerola (where the whole area looked very run down; like one of those 'high rise horrors from the 70's...which of course, it is) through Mijas, Marbella, Puerto Banus and Estepona.

Apparently, in the area between Nerja and Estepona (both of which are part of the district of Marbella) there are 40 golf courses! Recycled sea water is used to keep the greens looking....well, green.

We had a half hour stop at a service station before arriving at the border crossing and it was just as well because we had a long wait. It seems that the Spanish sometimes like to keep people waiting at the border into Gibraltar and of course, there is quite a lot of traffic for one small border point. The longest delay I heard of was four hours.

There was quite a long queue when we arrived, mostly cars but several coaches as well. Coaches don't have priority so we just had to sit there and wait our turn. After about half an hour, during which the coach hadn't moved at all, the tour guides and drivers from both Thomson coaches got their heads together and decided that the best thing to do, was for the passengers to disembark and cross the border on foot.

The drivers would have to stay with their coaches and wait it out. We didn't need them for the tour because there were mini buses waiting for us at the other side. So that's what we did; we all got off the coach with our passports and belongings and headed to the border on foot.

Crossing wasn't much of a problem, apart from one young couple from our coach who were turned back because the girl had a Moroccan passport. Not surprising really as she was from Morocco. No explanation was given and the tour guide had to arrange for a taxi to take the couple back to Torremolinos.

We had been told that mini buses would be waiting for us over the border but no-one said where. We all funnelled out of the building and along a narrow pathway and emerged onto the main road, Winston Churchill Avenue.

There were dozens and dozens of people just milling about and lots of mini buses parked by the kerb. More mini buses were parked across the street and several others in a nearby car park but there was nothing to tell us which was which. No-one came to tell us where to go or what to do so some of us stayed where we were while others wandered up and down trying to find the right bus. It was a complete shambles.

It seemed to me to be very lax in terms of security. Normally border crossings are heavily guarded and tightly controlled and the authorities don't want crowds of people milling around. It didn't seem as though anyone was particularly concerned about us.

Eventually we heard someone shout "Just follow this lady" so like sheep – and for want of anything better to do – we all did just that. We walked about a hundred yards or so then someone from our coach asked if we were going on the shopping trip. We said no, we were going on the tour.

"Oh, your mini bus is over there in the car park, on your right" she said. We turned around again and went back to where we'd started and more by good luck than good management, we found three mini buses in the car park, opposite the entrance to border control.

If our fellow traveller hadn't pointed us in the right direction we'd probably still be there!

Shortly afterwards, the rest of our group arrived and we set off on our whistle-stop tour of Gibraltar.

Our driver for the afternoon was also our guide. He spoke excellent English with a Spanish accent and just a touch of the "I say, old chap. Tally ho". Whenever he referred to the Royal Engineers – which he often did – he pronounced it 'enginairs'. He was very funny.

As he drove us around he gave us a lot of information about the area. The British Army arrived in Gibraltar in 1704 (some of them are dead now) and they set about building a huge defensive wall around the city, although in more recent times some of the land has been reclaimed, so that the port and some of the main industries are located outside the city wall.

Most of the original buildings are not only still standing but are still in use and have been well-maintained. There are lots of narrow, cobbled streets and narrow winding roads and I thought it was a really nice place.

I was particularly keen on the airport runway (there's only one) which is actually owned by the Ministry of Defence. It stretches across a narrow strip of land between the Mediterranean and the Atlantic and is just big enough to allow a 737 to land and take off but nothing larger than a 737.

Evidently it's one of the top five most dangerous airport runways in the world and I found it really strange that people can actually walk or drive across it. When an aircraft is about to land or take off, an alarm sounds and barriers are lowered to prevent people from crossing. It's the same idea as a level crossing for trains.

Our first stop on the tour was at Europa Point, where the Atlantic and Mediterranean meet. To the right is Spain and to the left is North Africa, specifically Morocco. Tarifa on the south coast of Spain, is also the most southerly point in Europe and is only about eight miles from Tangiers in North Africa. Both names became synonymous with the French Foreign Legion.

There is a mosque at Europa Point which was paid for and donated by King Fahad of Saudi Arabia. It cost £4 million but as his personal fortune was estimated at $150 billion, I don't suppose he missed it.

After admiring the view and taking some photographs, we resumed our journey. A little while later we stopped for about twenty minutes to meet some of Gibraltar's most famous residents; the Barbary Apes.

The apes originally came from Africa and live quite happily in small family groups on the Rock. They tend not to stay too close together because they fight, being very territorial. The point at which we stopped has five family groups but there are others further up the rock and more inaccessible. The latter group is said to be 'more wicked' because they aren't used to seeing many tourists.

Our little groups didn't seem to mind us being there and they sat pretty still, happy to pose for a photo shoot. They were clearly used to tourists and seemed quite bored by the experience. We weren't allowed to touch them or feed them but they let us approach quite close.

Having once again admired the view and taken more photographs, we headed back the few yards to our mini bus. We approached a group of four or five people who had been standing talking and all of a sudden, a chunk of rock about five inches by four inches and quite thick, landed in the middle of the group!

We all got a shock and, looking round to see where the rock had come from, we saw two or three apes sitting together on a bank behind us. We had all been so busy looking at the apes on the wall in front of us that we hadn't noticed there were any behind us.

It was the smallest ape in the group that had deliberately picked up a rock and thrown it at the group. As we looked over, one of the other apes turned away with a sort of "Nothing to do with me" expression while the small one was trying its hardest to pull up a large clump of soil and weeds. No doubt if it had succeeded, this would have been the next missile to be launched at us.

It was lucky that the first rock hadn't hit anyone; it would have certainly caused a nasty injury. As it was, it landed in the middle of the group. Had it hit the mini bus next to where the group was standing, it would probably have shattered the window.

It seemed like a good time to leave the apes to their own business and move off on the next leg of our journey.

Our next stop was to visit a series of interconnected, man-made tunnels which had originally been dug out by the good old Royal 'Enginairs' and then further extended during World War 2. They served as barracks, ammunition and fuel stores and perfect vantage points. The view from one of the 'windows' over the forces base, the airfield and out to sea was amazing.

The tunnels are high and wide and therefore I had no problem with my claustrophobia, although there was a dodgy moment when the guide told us that there was 140 feet of solid rock above our heads! I'd had happier thoughts!

We all had to wear safety helmets to avoid injury if anyone's head collided at speed with a piece of rock jutting out from the walls. Fortunately, the helmets came in a selection of colours. I selected a rather fetching pink one.

Our guide through the labyrinth was excellent. Not only did he really know his stuff but he was very enthusiastic and as soon as he started to speak it was obvious that he's been in the forces. He was a career soldier, a corporal who had retired in 2012. He was also a Londoner.

He led us through the tunnels, most of which had been named after streets or people and they had name plates on the walls, like street signs.

We were shown where the 'ordinary soldiers' were billeted and where the officers' quarters were, as well as the bakery, the mess and the storage areas. There was even a fire engine! There was also a small area set out like an office with a couple of typewriters dating from the war and on the walls were black and white photos showing the men eating, resting and working.

The soldiers who used to be based there worked eight hours a day digging out the tunnels then had eight hours of guard duty, leaving another eight hours to have their meals and sleep. They worked six days a week and were only allowed to shower on Sundays.......in cold water.

Some of us had a little taste of what it was like to have a cold shower because drops of water would drip onto us as we stood listening to our guide. A particularly large drop hit me on the nose at one point and I found myself wondering how many millennia that drop had been winding its way through the Jurassic limestone yet it chose that particular moment to drop on me.

Our tour through the tunnels lasted about 45 minutes and it was really interesting, thanks in no small way to our excellent guide. A memorable visit.

We headed to the commercial centre of Gibraltar to have a brief look around and to visit the shops. We had a coffee and a sandwich then waked along the main street. It was a narrow, pedestrianised area with bars, pavement cafes and lots of shops. The shops ranged from the touristy to the well-known brands.

There is a branch of Mothercare, Lloyds Bank, British Home Stores, Marks and Spencer and even the Newcastle Building Society! I spoke to one of the sales assistants in Marks and Spencer and it turned out that her mother was from Hebburn, about four miles away from where we live!

The money is the good old Pound Sterling but shops also accept the Euro.

I would have liked more time to look around but unfortunately, our coach was waiting in the car park to take us back over the border to Spain. We found out later that it had taken three hours for our driver to cross from Spain into Gibraltar.

We crossed the border on foot again, while our driver left by a separate exit. We rejoined our driver on the other side of the border and it was a much quicker process leaving than it was arriving.

Our 2 ½ hour drive took us through some beautiful scenery and it gave us the opportunity to experience the Spanish countryside.

I really enjoyed our visit to Gibraltar. The people we met were friendly, there's a lot to see and some great views. A little bit of Britain in Europe. Definitely worth a visit.

The mosque at Europa Point, Gibraltar

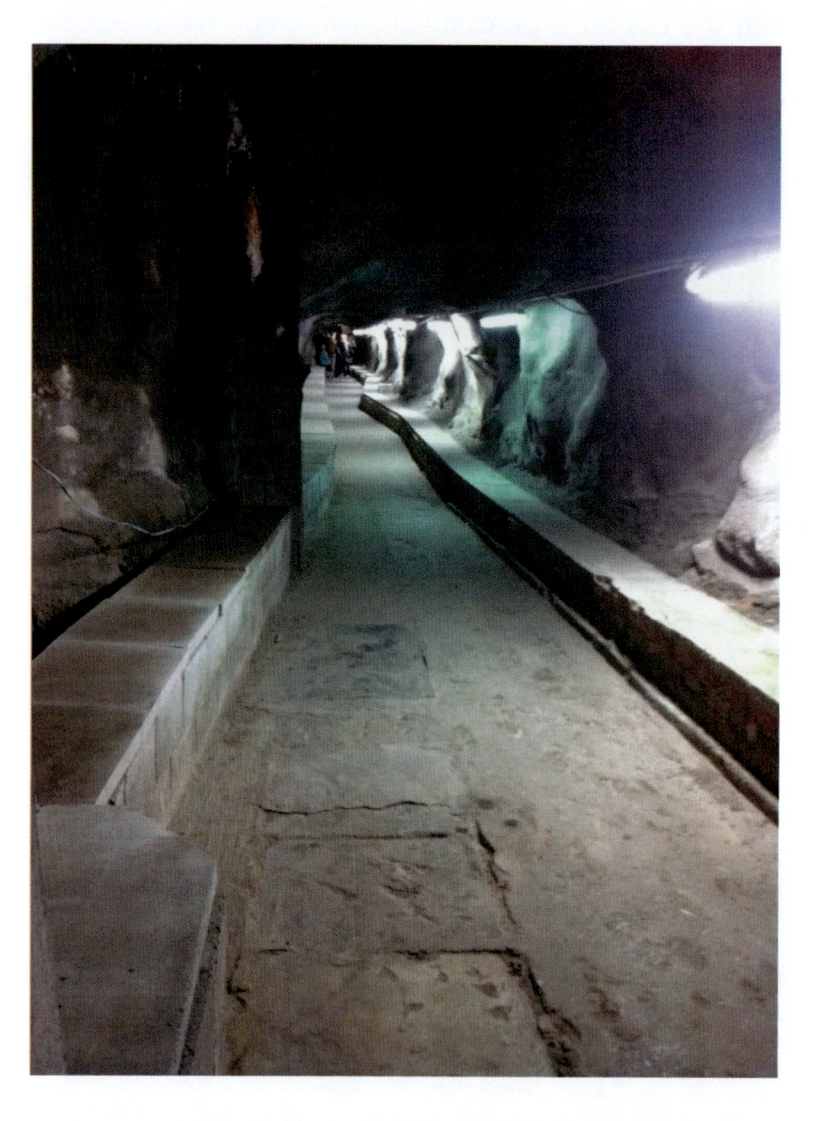

The tunnels dug by the Royal Engineers

One of the many Barbary Apes on Gibraltar.

British Forces base on Gibraltar.

Fire engine in the rock tunnels on Gibraltar

Chapter 7   Amsterdam

'Travelling is my drug of choice'.   *(Anonymous)*

One of the most popular 'short stay' locations is the city of Amsterdam. There is a regular ferry service from the River Tyne and it's popular with all ages. I knew a number of people who had made the trip and they all said they had enjoyed it. When my daughter came back from one such trip, she was very enthusiastic. She told us how much there was to see and do and said she'd definitely go back.

It seemed to be a bargain, too, with return ferry crossing (two nights on board), dinner on Friday and Saturday evenings and breakfast on Saturday and Sunday mornings all for £253 for two people. We booked with DFDS Seaways and travelled on the MS Queen of Scandanavia.

Katherine picked us up at 3pm and drove us through the Tyne Tunnel to the ferry landing, giving us a rundown of where to go and what to see. She stayed with us until we checked in. She then headed back through the Tunnel so she could be back at South Shields seafront in time to wave us off when we left the river.

I was pleasantly surprised when we boarded the ship; being a ferry I had expected it to be rather basic and functional, even a bit drab but reception was quite welcoming. There was a wide staircase which gave access to the rest of the ship. Our cabin (4028) was on reception level, deck four and we were at the 'blunt' end, which my husband insisted that we call 'the stern'.

I had to 'bow' to his superior knowledge in that regard as he had spent 25 years working on ships in various shipyards along the Tyne.

Our cabin was larger than I had expected, with a decent sized window (sorry, porthole) and plenty of space.

It was quite cloudy when we left the ferry terminal and by the time we reached the river mouth it was raining heavily. Even so, we went up on deck and saw Katherine standing exactly where she said she would be, waving frantically. We waved back but we didn't know whether she could pick us out from the others on the deck from that distance.

We went to our cabin to shower and change and then headed to the restaurant on deck 8. The meal was excellent and there was plenty of choice; lots of seafood and salads, jacket potatoes, various meats, lots of desserts....it was all very nice. Meals were all buffet service.

There were lots of activities on board; cabaret, a cinema, bingo, a couple of bars, children's activities and even horse-racing, though not with real horses of course; the ship wasn't quite that big.

From our cabin I could see the east coast of England in the distance, which I suppose meant that we were on the starboard side of the ship. I hadn't expected to be sailing so far down the coast before turning and heading east towards Holland. Memories of that famous 'Only Fools and Horses' sketch flashed into my mind; follow the ferry and if you get lost, ask directions from a man on an oil rig platform!

It was quite a windy evening but the sea wasn't too rough, although as we were sailing against the direction of the waves, every now and then a wave would hit the bow in such a way as to give us a bit of a lurch but actually, there was very little sense of movement.

Ship's time was an hour ahead of UK time so at 11pm we decided to try and get some sleep as we had an early start the following morning. I didn't really sleep much; a strange bed, unfamiliar noises and the ever present realisation that we were in the middle of the North Sea, all conspired to give me a restless night.

After an early – and excellent – breakfast the next morning, we disembarked at 9am and went through Passport Control. It was surprising how many people seemed unaware that we were in a foreign country and they would need their passports. They had to rush back to their cabins for them.

I often wonder why we need a passport with 30 pages when so many countries don't bother to stamp them now.

Outside there was a lady directing us to our coaches. Some people were heading straight into the city while others had opted for the sightseeing tour first. We had elected to do the sightseeing tour and driving in from the ferry terminal, I was quite impressed with how green the place was, even the industrial estates had lawns and plants and trees.

Many of the modern buildings seemed to be low-rise and they fitted in pretty well with the older ones. I must admit to being pleasantly surprised because Amsterdam has a bit of a reputation and I expected it to be a bit seedy but it wasn't like that at all.

Like so many places across the world, Amsterdam was once a small fishing village and it dates back to the 12th century. It shares a border with Germany and Belgium and was once the site of the dam over the River Amstel, which is how it got its name. Originally a Catholic country, Amsterdam revolted against the Spanish rule of the Netherlands in 1578 and became a Protestant country.

Amsterdam is the Dutch capital of the Netherlands and has a population of 81,000 within the city limits.

We drove past the Reichs Museum (which was closed when we were there because the authorities had found asbestos in the building) and the Science Museum, a modern monstrosity which the locals refer to as 'The Titanic' because it looks like a sinking ship.

Amsterdam was home to the young World War 2 diarist Anne Frank and it is possible to visit her house. Another famous resident was the troubled painter, Vincent Van Gogh and there is a museum dedicated to him and his work.

We arrived in the city itself about 11am and walked up the wide main street, past the famous Krasnapolsky Hotel, the Kroninklijk Palace, the National Monument and Madame Tussauds and eventually we arrived at the flower market, also known as the floating flower market.

The market floats on a series of barges but most visitors aren't aware of it as it sits so well in the street scene. There are 15 stalls which are open all year, Monday to Saturday, 9am to 6pm and the market itself (known locally as the 'Bloemenmarket') dates back to 1862.

It really is beautiful and a 'must see' for anyone travelling to the area. The smells, the colours, the variety of plants, flowers and floral arrangements are quite spectacular. The prices were very reasonable, too. We paid 8 Euros (about £5) for a bunch of 50 yellow tulips.

We spent the rest of the afternoon wandering up and down narrow streets and criss-crossing the canals, being very careful to avoid the thousands of bicycles that swarm like insects all over the city's 250 miles of cycleways.

We walked through attractive, shaded squares where people were sitting reading newspapers, chatting or listening to street musicians. It was a lovely, warm and sunny day and there were a lot of people out enjoying the weather. I loved the old buildings, the little bridges over the canals, the tree-lined and litter-free streets and the pavement cafes.

We had of course, been told about the 'other kind' of cafes for which Amsterdam is famous and where – due to the rather more liberal drug laws – cannabis and cannabis products can be sold from licenced coffee shops.

The coffee shops are not allowed to openly advertise so there is usually a cannabis plant in the window or a picture of one on the door. These cafes are not allowed to sell alcohol or any other kind of drug and in fact, in other parts of the Netherlands they can refuse to serve tourists but not in Amsterdam itself.

The tour guide on our coach – whilst not advocating that any of us should try cannabis – was sufficiently 'savvy' to realise that some tourists will do just that, so she gave us a few words of warning, should we wish to sample the dubious delights of one of the 'brown cafes'.

There is a saying about these places, that you walk in but you fly out!

Most will have a 'speciality of the house', which are referred to as 'pot brownies', 'space cakes', 'space muffins' or 'hash brownies' (definitely not to be confused with the hash browns you might have for breakfast!)

The cakes and cookies can be of any kind and cannabis is the extra ingredient. You won't find these in the Be-Ro book! They cause – I'm told – a 'pleasant high' which can last for several hours but which can leave a feeling of drowsiness or detachment the next day.

'Space cakes' cost around 4 or 5 Euros each and on no account should they be taken before, after or with alcohol because the combination can make people pass out cold and many have been hospitalised as a result.

I have to say that even when Jimmy pointed out the pungent small emanating from several of these 'brown cafes', I couldn't smell it so I still don't know what cannabis smells like. At one point, we were sitting on a bench next to a young man and after about ten minutes, Jimmy said we'd have to move or he'd be as high as a kite. Apparently the young man had been smoking the old 'Moroccan Woodbine' and I hadn't even noticed!

We had a nice lunch and then ended up walking down a narrow street which led to the Red Light district. We hadn't intended to go there but at least now I can say I've seen it.

This liberal aspect of the city is also regulated. There are 300 single room cabins and owners must display the required health certificates to show that the premises have been inspected. The ladies must be 21 years old or over and must undergo regular health checks at the government's expense. 75% of the women are Asian, African or Eastern European.

Street prostitution is not permitted and there are no 'pimps'.

Things were very quiet when we were there; actually it made me feel quite uncomfortable. Apart from an extremely thin, blonde lady and an older woman who could possibly have been Jabba the Hutt's mother, the rest of the girls must have been on their lunch break!

Oh and in case you're curious, the cost at that time was 30 Euros, which was about £21 in real money.

I think we got a better deal at the flower market!

Eventually we boarded one of the shuttle buses to return to the ferry terminal. The journey takes about half an hour, depending on traffic and as taxis are very expensive, it's advisable to leave plenty of time for the return journey.

When we arrived, we discovered that passengers couldn't board the ship until 5pm so we all had to sit in a small, hot, cramped departure area while coach after coach deposited more and more people. Quite a few passengers were smoking (just tobacco, as far as anyone could determine) but hadn't the sense to go outside to smoke so we were all suffocating by the time we 5 o'clock came around.

Once the ship had left the ferry terminal, we went to our cabin to shower and change, then we had a drink in the bar before having a late dinner. Again, the meal was excellent.

We were woken up at 7.15 the following morning by an announcement over the tannoy asking if there was a doctor on board. Apparently the ferry crew are first aid trained but if something more serious happens, the options are to wait until the ferry arrives in port and have an ambulance waiting or to fly a doctor out to the ship by helicopter.

Later we saw a helicopter circling the ship three or four times and it looked as though it might be going to winch someone off the ship but it left without doing so. When we arrived in port, Katherine said she had heard that there had been a death on board, which I suppose would explain why no-one was airlifted from the ship.

Katherine drove us home the long way round so she could park at the site of the former Redheads Shipyard and we could see the whole ship from the opposite side of the river.

I was really impressed with Amsterdam; it was much nicer than I had expected. There is so much to see and do that – like Gibraltar – one day doesn't really do it justice.

One thing we didn't have time to do was to take one of the popular canal trips but perhaps that's an option for a future visit.

The Krasnapolsky Hotel, Amsterdam

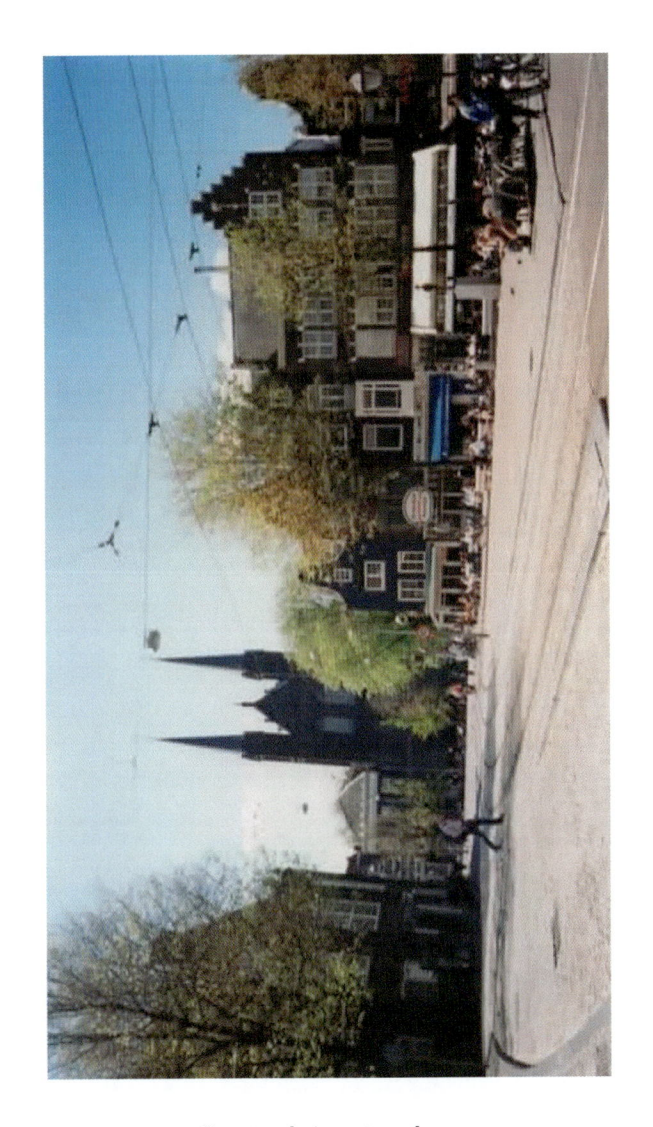

Central Amsterdam

The flower market, Amsterdam

Chapter 8   Fuerteventura

'A vacation is having nothing to do and all day to do it in'.
(Robert Orsen)

There's very little that puts me on edge more than having to be up at stupid o'clock to be somewhere at a certain time. I am not and never have been, an early morning person. It's even worse when I've actually managed to get up early then the taxi is late and I'm waiting around when I could have had another ten minutes in bed!

September 19th 2000 at 5.30am we were waiting for a taxi that should have picked us up at 5.15. It finally arrived at 5.40 and we had a pretty hair-raising journey to Newcastle Airport.

There was a new International Departures check-in area and having stood in the queue only about 15 minutes, the process itself took very little time. We were staying in a Thomson Platinum hotel so our boarding cards for the return flight were issued at the same time as those for the outbound flight and our cases would be checked in at our hotel on the day of departure.

We hadn't been in the departure lounge very long when we were called to board our Britannia flight to Fuerteventura. Our journey took us out over Birmingham first, then Cardiff, across the west coast of France then via central Spain to the Canary Islands, specifically Fuerteventura.

We were advised by the captain that there was a strong head wind so the journey was expected to last 4 hours and 20 minutes. Of course, the Canary Islands are very close to Africa (Fuerteventura is only about 62 miles away); it normally takes us the same amount of time to fly from Gatwick to Luxor.

Tourism came to Fuerteventura in the 1960's (the first hotel opened in 1965) and the large scale developments in the 1980's increased tourism significantly.

Fuerteventura is the oldest island in the Canary Island chain, having been created around 20 million years ago and at 641 square miles, it is the second largest after Tenerife. Tenerife is also the most active, volcanically speaking, whereas the last volcanic activity on Fuerteventura took place between 4,000 and 5,000 years ago.

The name 'Fuerteventura' means 'strong wind' and the conditions make it ideal for sailing and surfing and the wind keeps the temperatures bearable. It is also well known as a good diving area. The beaches are white sand or black shingle or sometimes a mixture of both.

The earliest settlement on the island and its first capital, was Betancuria but the modern capital is Puerto del Rosario. The island has a population of around 75,000.

The journey from the airport to the hotel took about an hour and the landscape we drove through was very stark and barren but impressive, nevertheless. I could understand why they chose to film 'Planet of the Apes' here (the original and better version, starring Roddy McDowell).

Our first impressions of the hotel were very favourable. The Jandia (pronounced 'Handia') Princess had a central building which housed reception, bars, restaurants and shops then there were two 'wings' of three -storey blocks which housed all the guest rooms. The blocks were terraced so that the balconies didn't overlook each other or block the views from other rooms.

We were in room 6314; block 6, floor 3 and we had a great view of the Atlantic Ocean.

The grounds were well laid out and contained lots of narrow, winding paths with some very attractive features. There was a very nice pool area with plenty of sun loungers, from which staff were authorised to remove any towels, books or other items that had been left unattended for some time.

Around 80% of holiday-makers on the island are German and after Spanish, German is the most commonly spoken language.

A couple of days after we arrived, we decided to have a walk to the beach, which was about a quarter of a mile from the hotel…..straight down! We had to walk along a couple of the little winding paths, through a door and down a two-tier ramp and finally, down a very long flight of steps to the beach itself.

Well, walking down was one thing but coming back was a real test of stamina and endurance!

The sea was a mixture of patches of dark blue and turquoise and it was cold. The sand was a mixture of regular sand and black sand and there were lots of black, volcanic rocks strewn all over the beach. They ranged in size from small pebbles to huge boulders.

Jandia is a small area but it is the second largest resort on the island. There is a market in town on Thursdays between 9.30am and 1.30pm. Getting there in a taxi from the hotel only took about ten minutes and in the days before the Euro, cost about 700 Pesetas.

The alternative route is along the beach and this takes about 45 minutes each way.

The beach is both a nudist and non-nudist beach, there is no segregation and no signs to warn the unwary and unsuspecting traveller.

Why is it that most nudists seem to weight about 27 stone? I saw one woman who was the nearest thing I'd ever seen to perpetual motion; not only did everything move but it kept on moving! Of course, trying to avoid looking at the nudists meant that we ended up looking into middle distance, thereby tripping over many of those rocks and boulders I mentioned.

The nearer we got to town, we noticed the beach filling up considerably so we were glad our hotel was some distance away. The town itself was small; really just one street with a couple of bars, some shops and a supermarket. It might have grown since then.

We stocked up on some essentials – Diet Coke, wine, beer – because wherever we are in the world, we always like to sit on our balcony and have a drink while watching the sunset before changing for dinner.

The Sunday after our arrival we had arranged to take a day trip to Lanzarote. It meant a very early start in order to catch the 9am ferry – which was quite a distance away – so we had to leave the hotel at 6.20am. Now, I only recognise one 6.20 a day and it's not that one!

The ferry crossing took about forty minutes and it gave us a great view of this volcanic island. Of course, all the Canary Islands are volcanic, having emerged from the sea millions of years ago. Although Tenerife is the most volcanically active, the most dangerous is said to be La Palma.

La Palma has one active volcano and one extinct one but in the same year we visited Fuerteventura, there was a theory put forward that the western flank of the Cumbre Vieja – already about 12 to 13 feet lower than the other flank – would one day slide into the ocean. This would create a mega-tsunami of such height and strength that it would cross the ocean and wipe out much of the eastern seabord of the United States. Of course, this might not happen for thousands of years, if at all.

Immediately, other scientists rushed to deny the claims, pointing out amongst other things, that there hadn't been an Atlantic mega-tsunami in recorded history (so what?) and that the layout and structure of the Atlantic made it almost impossible for a tsunami to cross the Atlantic. An underwater landslide off the nearby island of El Hierro in September 2011 has set everyone talking again.

Meanwhile, back on Lanzarote, we were accompanied on our journey by our driver Pedro and our guide, Roger. Roger was originally from Bradford and had lived on Fuerteventura for nine years. His wife – who was the guide on the second coach – was from Scotland.

As we journeyed through the red and brown Martian landscape of the island, we learnt that there were two types of lava, both of which have Hawaiian names. The very thick, viscous, molten rock is called 'A'a' and the more fluid, liquid type has the wonderful name of 'pa hoey hoey' (pronounced phonetically).

The last eruption on Lanzarote was on February 1st 1730 but as the volcanoes are very similar to the ones on Hawaii and tend not to be the explosive kind, people were able to evacuate the area successfully.

We arrived at our first destination of the day and for my money, the best: Timanfaya National Park. The incredible landscape is the result of volcanic activity and consists of deep craters, lave tubes, caves and precipitous peaks with rocks and boulders scattered everywhere. It was an amazing site and difficult to imagine if you haven't seen it.

The National Park covers an area of 19.72 square miles and was declared a biosphere by UNESCO in 1993. Access is strictly regulated. The area takes its name from the only remaining active volcano on the island, Timanfaya.

While we were there, we had several demonstrations of the awesome power of nature contained – at least for now – deep underground.

We all stood in a semi-circle behind a line drawn with a spade in the gravel and we were invited to touch the gravel at our feet. It was cold. We were then asked to put our fingers into the gravel, as though making a hole to plant something. This time - and only an inch or so below the surface - the gravel was hot.

Finally, one of the park rangers dug down just a couple of feet with his spade and put a small amount of the gravel he had dug out into our hands. After a second or two we had to drop it because it was red hot!

The second demonstration involved the ranger pouring a ladle of cold water into a small blowhole and seconds later, a jet of steam gushed out of the blowhole with such force that it made us all jump!

Next another of the rangers pushed a piece of prickly bush into a narrow but deep vent and within seconds, smoke appeared from the vent and almost immediately after that, the bush burst into flames!

Nature at its primitive and powerful best.

In the nearby restaurant there was a small circular room which was open to the sky and which had a retaining wall around a deep pit. The pit was perhaps thirty feet deep and over the top of it was a metal grille. It seemed to be used as a kind of barbecue. The retaining wall itself was about waist height and we could peer over the edge, being careful to secure our hats, cameras and spectacles first.

Very hot air was rising from the pit and now and then, a blast of even hotter air. It was amazing.

I found the whole area fascinating. The scenery and the landscape were spectacular; strange, primitive and alien but quite breath-taking.

When we left the National Park, we headed to a 'bodega' where grapes are grown and wine produced. The vines grow along the ground so that they don't snap in the wind and they are protected by horseshoe-shaped stone shelters.

Grapes are harvested on the Canary Islands earlier than elsewhere but because of the labour-intensive way they are grown and harvested, the wine is quite expensive.

We sampled three wines; a dry white (which I normally prefer), a red and a semi-sweet white and I was surprised to find that I liked the semi-sweet Muscatel the best. It wasn't really a table wine but as a small glass of dessert wine it would be perfect.

The wines cost 900 Pesetas a bottle so I bought a bottle of each one we'd tried.

One of the by-products of volcanic activity is the beautiful, lime-green, semi-precious stone known as the 'peridot' and conveniently located next door to the bodega was a workshop, where the stones were fashioned into items of jewellery and sold.

Yes, I bought a ring. It was in sterling silver and I paid the equivalent of £39 for it.

Pedro then drove us to Teguise to look around and visit the market that takes place every Sunday.

Teguise is the oldest Spanish settlement in the Canary Islands and dates back to 1402. For 450 years, it was the island's capital and was a favourite target of the pirates that used to prowl the seas in this region. In 1618, the town was attacked by 5,000 Algerian pirates who massacred many of the local people. This barbaric act is commemorated in a small street called La Sangre, meaning 'blood'.

The street is next to the town's main church, Nuestro Senora de Guadaloupe.

After lunch we went to a vantage point called Mirador del Rios from which we enjoyed magnificent views.

Our final stop of the day was at the 'Jameos del Agua', the 'Caves of Water'. This is in fact, a lava tube created by nature but developed by man so that there are steps cut into the lave rock which lead to three small bars. At one point, visitors can look down and see the sea water at the bottom of the lava tube where it begins its one- mile journey to the Atlantic. Above sea level, the lava tube is four miles long and the 'roof' is about 45 feet high.

There is a small auditorium where visitors can sit and soak up the atmosphere whilst listening to strange, ethereal music.

There is a deep underground pool in the cave and all over the rocks are what look like tiny white spots, which seemed to glow in the semi-darkness. These dots are in fact, a species of blind crab which is found nowhere else in the world. Not only are they unique to Lanzarote, they are unique to this particular cave. They are so tiny that unless visitors go right to the water's edge, the creatures are almost impossible to see.

There is something about a pool of water that makes humans want to throw coins in it but next to this particular pool was a sign telling visitors not to throw any coins into the water because the corrosion would kill the tiny crabs.

As we drove back to catch the six o'clock ferry to Fuerteventura, we reflected on some of the amazing sights we had seen in just a few hours.

Although we arrived back at the island at about ten to seven, the coach had a lot of 'drop off' points so we didn't actually get back to our hotel until 9 o'clock and we found a cold supper waiting for us.

Several days later, we went on another trip, this time around Fuerteventura itself and on the morning we were going, eight of us were sitting in the lobby at half past eight. We were supposed to have been collected at twenty past so we weren't worried at that point but when the coach still hadn't arrived ten minutes later, one of our group decided to have a look up the drive and sure enough, there was the coach waiting.

The driver had decided not to drive down the bank to the hotel entrance, as would normally be the case.

Our guide was called Thea and she was Dutch. She had been living on the island for eight years – as do many foreigners - mostly because it was 'stress free', according to Thea. Well, that may be but there are other things to consider; water is in short supply, the island is dry and barren with very little vegetation and the villages tend to be quite isolated from each other.

Apparently, many Canary Islanders emigrate to other parts of the world, particularly South America. The Mayor of one of the villages on Lanzarote was one such emigrant. In 1729, he took a number of villagers with him to the 'New World' and they founded the city of San Antonio in Texas.

Fuerteventura's popularity with the Germans stemmed from the end of the Second World War, when a German architect was given a large quantity of land and he built Jandia.

Before he left, he gave some of the land back but until the late 1990's, Germans were still able to buy land and property very cheaply. Many Germans still live in and around Jandia.

Of course, prices have risen to such an extent that islanders cannot afford to buy land and property on their own island! Sadly, this happens all over the world once tourists move in.

Around 80% of islanders rely on tourism for their livelihoods.

We learnt from Thea that it was only recently that education had become compulsory from the age of six and that many older people on the island could neither read nor write.

On Fuerteventura, when people become frail or unable to look after themselves, they usually go to live with their children, grandchildren or other relatives so there was only one residential home for older people on the island; it is located in the capital, Puerto del Rosario.

The first place we visited on our tour was Paraja, which is in the south west of the island and has a population of around 21,000. We had a look around the little church of Nuestra de Regia, which has carvings of snakes, birds and panthers at the entrance. This has led some to speculate that there are links with the Mayan or Aztec cultures.

We travelled on to Betancuria, once the island's capital. The main attraction for visitors is the church of Santa Maria, which was built in 1405. The church was destroyed by pirates in 1593 and gradually rebuilt over the next hundred years.

On the way back to the hotel, we stopped for a little while to admire the magnificent sand dunes at Corralejo then visited a tiny, out of the way spot to enjoy what Thea called 'special coffee'. The coffee was served with cream and a local honey liqueur and it was delicious.

We arrived back at the hotel at 5.30, plenty of time to shower and change and have a drink on the balcony before dinner.

One surprise attraction on the island turned out to be Jimmy's favourite and we discovered it quite by accident.

We were returning from a walk along the beach and at the bottom of the steps leading up to the hotel, there was a sort of stone 'rotunda'. Two people were standing next to it and holding out their hands. It looked like some sort of ritual but as we got closer, we were amazed to find that the wall was crawling with chipmunks!

These lovely, tiny creatures looked like small squirrels and they were eating monkey nuts out of the couple's hands. The chipmunks were peering out of almost every crevice in the rock and running all over!

We spoke to the couple – it turned out that he was from Gateshead, about eight miles from where we live – and they gave us some monkey nuts so we could feed the chipmunks, too. The animals would take the nuts from our hands and stand eating them. We stood there for about half an hour and ended up going back every day for the remainder of the holiday.

At the end of our two weeks, the rep asked us what had been our favourite part of the holiday. I said mine was Timanfaya National Park. Jimmy said his was feeding the chipmunks!

On our last day, we had the 'privilege' of checking in for our flight whilst we were still at the hotel because were on a Platinum holiday. Those of you who have been paying close attention will recall that when we checked in at Newcastle for our outbound flight, we were given the boarding cards for our return journey. We were supposed to be in row 34.

At the hotel, we had to check in again and we were issued with new boarding cards by the Iberian Airlines rep! So what was the point of checking us in and giving us boarding cards at Newcastle?

When we left the hotel we had an hour's journey to get to the airport. Even though the airport building had only been built five years earlier and was pretty modern, no-one seemed to have given any thought to the fact that there were only two cashiers desks in the Duty Free shop. Long queues soon built up and the people in the queues were impeding those who were trying to reach the shelves to make their purchases.

I checked the information screen and it advised that our flight – which had been due to leave at 12.55 – would now be leaving at 12.25 and would be boarding at gate 2. I checked again about 15 minutes later only to discover that our flight would in fact, be boarding from gate 4.

Jimmy and I sat chatting for a while then I checked the board again. This time our boarding gate would be number 10. We grabbed our hand luggage and dashed along to the other end of the departure lounge to discover that the flight wasn't boarding at all at that point. Shortly afterwards, our flight was called and we boarded ……..by a completely different gate.

I think it was all a game to prevent us from being bored in the departure lounge.

Things were a bit chaotic because not only were all the passengers boarding at once but we were all boarding only via the front steps. Our 12.25 departure ended up being 1.10.

We had lots of time to relax on holiday. The hotel was quite a long way out of the town but for us, that's usually a good thing.

We saw a great deal of Fuerteventura and saw some amazing sights on Lanzarote so it gave us the best of both worlds really; sightseeing and relaxation. Just what holidays are for.

Feeding the chipmunks at Jandia

The Jandia Princess, Fuerteventura

Blowing off steam, Lanzarote

Timanfaya National Park, Lanzarote

Timanfaya Volcano, Lanzarote

So where to next?

I hope you've enjoyed this little 'taster' of some of the places we've been lucky enough to travel to. I also hope it might have encouraged you to visit some of them and see for yourself what they have to offer and to learn about the places; the history, the culture, the people.

There are some spectacular sights and scenery to enjoy, too, so my advice would be, go out and explore; you might be surprised at what you find.

'Travel. As much as you can. As far as you can. As long as you can. Life's not meant to be lived in one place.'
(Will Smith)

There will be other books in this series; two about Egypt, one about Florida and another 'multi-destination' one, which will contain chapters about Madeira, Malta, Spain, Tunisia, Mexico, Crete and Porto Santo. I hope you'll join me on these journeys, too.

In the meantime, I don't think I can put it any better than the immortal Mark Twain, who said:

"Twenty years from now you'll regret the things you didn't do far more than the things you did. So throw off the bowlines, sail away from safe harbour, catch the Trade Winds in your sails. Explore. Dream. Discover."

Happy travelling!

References and photo credits

'A Brief History of the Passport'. The Guardian, Nov. 17th 2006

'A Brief History of the Package Holiday'. The Guardian, June 14th 2013

'A Brief History of Holidays'.   Tim Lambert

'The Golden Age of Travel'   Andrew Williamson

'Flight to the Sun'   Roger Bray

Photo of the 7 coloured earth at Chamarel by 'Moongateclimber'

Photo of Timanfaya volcano by Jose A. Duarte Llorente

Post cards of Cap d'Agde and Grau d'Agde by kind permission of the local tourist board.

……and of course, good old Google and Wikipedia, both of which saved me from days of trawling through reference books.

booksbyally@outlook.com

Printed in Great Britain
by Amazon.co.uk, Ltd.,
Marston Gate.